Leadership, Higher Education, and the Information Age

A New Era for Information Technology and Libraries

Edited by Carrie E. Regenstein and Barbara I. Dewey

Neal-Schuman Publishers, Inc.
New York London

Published by Neal-Schuman Publishers, Inc.
100 Varick Street
New York, NY 10013

Printed and bound in the United States of America.

The paper used in this publication meets the minimum requirements of American National Standard for Information Sciences—Permanence of Paper for Printed Library Materials, ANSI Z39.48—1992 ♾

Library of Congress Cataloging-in-Publication Data

Leadership, higher education, and the information age : a new era for information technology and libraries / edited by Carrie E. Regenstein, Barbara I. Dewey.

p. cm.

Includes bibliographical references and index.

ISBN 1-55570-455-7 (alk. paper)

1. Education, Higher—United States—Effect of technological innovations on. 2. Educational technology—United States—Planning. 3. Information technology—United States—Planning. 4. Computer-assisted instruction—United States—Planning. 5. Academic libraries—Automation—Management. I. Regenstein, Carrie. II. Dewey, Barbara I.

LB1028.3.L375 2003
378'.00285'4—dc21

2002032589

Contents

IV: DEVELOPING NEW LEADERSHIP

Preface

The title *Leadership, Higher Education, and the Information Age: A New Era for Information Technology and Libraries* was coined before the cataclysmic events of September 2001—events that transported us into yet another "new era." This new era requires new leadership. Leaders in both the private and public sectors—including those who have written about higher education in these chapters—are therefore rethinking definitions, strategies, and personal expectations for success.

Definitions for "leader"—like "guide" or "conductor"—are only a beginning; more accurate definitions also include vision, passion, commitment, and courage. Leadership is at once "of the individual" and "of the community," intellectually challenging, and emotionally demanding. It is both intentional and serendipitous; it is thrilling and it is hard work. Leadership must be informed and compassionate. On good days it is joyful. Our hope is that readers will discover new perspectives, strategies, and inspiration to support their own growth and contributions as leaders in higher education.

What's working in higher education? What needs to be done differently or better? Where do we need to help steer our institutions? How do we demonstrate our respectfulness of multiple cultures while moving the enterprise forward? And what kinds of leaders must we become to make our institutions more effective in the future? *Leadership, Higher Education, and the Information Age: A New Era for Information Technology and Libraries* explores new paths in scholarship and institutional management that involve information technology organizations and libraries.

Part I, "Seeing a Wider View," explores the development of

new visions and strategies for higher education institutions. In the first chapter, "Developing a Campus-Wide Vision for Use of Information Technology," Renee Drabier provides both a broad overview of the challenge of strategic planning and visioning and specific recommendations for success. Chapter 2, "Designing IT Strategic Planning for the Smaller Institution," by Patrick Kohrman and Dennis Trinkle, provides a complementary view with a focus on smaller institutions, detailing the steps involved in the process. As educational offerings increasingly become available beyond the bounds of time and space, it is critical to consider our strategies in functional rather than institutional terms. To this end, Lois Brooks provides her overview, "Finding the Vision: Shaping Technology Support Services in the Twenty-First Century Institution," the final chapter of Part I.

The practicalities of fulfilling the vision are explored in Part II, "Examining Cultural and Organizational Transformation." Given that leadership often requires the ability to influence without official authority, leadership in the new era also requires an understanding of and appreciation for artful negotiation within multiple cultures and biases. Anne Scrivener Agee and Dee Ann Holisky provide insights and guidance on collaborations between faculty and IT professionals in Chapter 4, "Crossing the Great Divide: Implementing Change by Creating Collaborative Relationships." Their experience at George Mason University was recognized with an EDUCAUSE Award for Systemic Progress in Teaching and Learning. In the fifth chapter, "Exploring Cultural Challenges to the Integration of Technology," Jo Ann Carr considers issues that emerge between teacher education and arts and sciences programs with respect to the integration of technology in teaching and learning in higher education. In Chapter 6, "Finding the Third Space: On Leadership Issues Related to the Integration of Library and Computing," Christopher Ferguson and Terry Metz offer insights and recommendations to leaders of new, emerging organizations created out of the merger between libraries and computing centers.

Since measurable progress is made by overcoming the challenges inherent in fulfilling grand visions, we detail two real-life applications of successful IT leadership in Part III as a reality check—and as an inspiration. The very expression "IT professional" belies the disparate talents, interests, and work styles found among the staff members in central and distributed campus IT organizations. In Chapter 7, "Transforming Technology Training: Partnerships, Packages, and Policies," Pattie Orr offers an example (and hope!) that multiple IT service units can and do collaborate in effective and efficient ways to serve students, faculty, and staff. And Vince Sheehan and Jay Fern offer an exciting story about implementing an e-learning initiative in Chapter 8, "Turning Coal into Diamonds: Organizing Under Pressure."

Leadership is both programmatic and personal. Robert Renaud and Anne Murray open Part IV, "Developing New Leadership," with a presentation of strategies librarians can use for becoming leaders—not simply managers—of higher education in Chapter 9, "Organizing for Leadership: How University Libraries Can Meet the Leadership Challenge in Higher Education." And *if* higher education seeks different leadership contributions from IT and library professionals, what new issues emerge when these entities are integrated on a campus? In Chapter 10, "Rising to the Top: The Peculiar Leadership Challenges for the Successful Internal Candidate," Elizabeth Hammond provides a candid perspective on leadership, focusing on the internal job candidate and his or her colleagues.

It is fitting to conclude this publication with an eye towards the future of the scholarly community as suggested in Part V, "Anticipating What's Next: Leadership for Digital Initiatives." In the final essay, Chapter 11, co-editor Barbara Dewey provides a vision of "Considering Leadership and the New Architecture for Digital Libraries."

In *The Mirage of Continuity: Reconfiguring Academic Education Information Resources for the 21st Century,* Patricia Batten wrote "Leaders of the transition—those who will make it happen at every level of the organization—will need acute powers of analysis, abundant common sense, vibrant creativity, reasoned judgment, and a passionate commitment to the mission and goals of the extended higher education community." I keep these words at hand for inspiration and guidance, and now look forward to supplementing them with additions from these essays. We invite readers to discover new perspectives that might be kept "close at hand" in the exciting and challenging times ahead.

CARRIE E. REGENSTEIN
University of Wisconsin-Madison

Part I

Seeing a Wider View

Chapter 1

Developing a Campuswide Vision for Use of Information Technology in Teaching and Learning

Renee Drabier
Chief Technology Officer and Director, Information Technology Services, University of Southern Colorado

OVERVIEW: THE CHALLENGE OF STRATEGIC PLANNING AND VISIONING IN HIGHER EDUCATION

Strategic planning has been championed as an important way to address the challenges faced by higher education (DeBard and Peck, 2000; Harvey, 1998; Yamada, 1991). Increasing pressures on the academy as a result of rising costs, accountability demands, and productivity pressures have contributed to a growing focus on strategic planning as an opportunity to transform and improve higher education institutions and to respond in an effective and innovative way to its environment and constituents (Korschen, Fuller, and Lambert, 2000). A review of strategic planning and visioning literature reveals that the great majority of what has been written addresses planning techniques most suitable for use by corporate America. Much of this literature does not address the special needs and considerations of successful planning in the complex environment of higher education. However, a growing body of literature that specifically addresses the special challenges involved in strategic planning for higher education is emerging. Rowley, Lujan, and Dolence (1997) produced an excellent guide in their *Strategic Change in Colleges and Universities* in which the focus is on techniques tailored for use in academic organizations to support the planning process to help the organization "survive and prosper."

Advances in technology are opening opportunities to increase access to education to new and underserved populations, to improve traditional educational delivery inside and outside of the classroom, and to allow colleges and universities to be competitive in an environment of rapidly emerging new educational providers and competitors. In an explanation of the barriers to higher education's moving forward faster to take advantage of opportunities and effect change, Billy E. Frye described the mission and purposes of U.S. colleges and universities as "generally very complex," resulting in institutions that have organized themselves in a "highly fragmented, compartmentalized, and autonomous way" (Frye, 2002: 10). These organizational structures increase the difficulty of bringing about major change and are barriers to an organization's responding in an effective and innovative way to its environment and constituents. Particular characteristics that also contribute to making planning in higher education especially challenging include the culture of shared governance, resistance to reallocation of resources, financial formulas, and the diversity of constituencies.

Korschgen, Fuller, and Lambert (2000) conducted a study of 27 institutions of higher education and formed a number of important conclusions regarding successful planning efforts, including:

top leadership must be involved with the planning process;
leaders must talk with all constituents to understand key issues;
leaders must have a deep understanding of the institution's culture, people, and history;

inclusion of many constituent voices, including established governance groups, is essential;
emphasis must be given to communicating the process and the resultant plans to internal and external constituencies;
planning must be linked to the institutional budgeting process.

The authors found that the most effective planning processes were tailor-made to the campuses, simple and focused, established broad themes concerning the direction of the institution, examined key resource and budget questions, and expected those responsible for carrying out the themes to fill in the details and execute the plans. The development of a campus-wide vision for use of technology that fits the mission and strategic directions of the institution is essential to guide actions, activities, expenditures, and information technology implementation. This alignment will improve the effectiveness and efficiency of the entire organization by focusing scarce resources in the areas that will most effectively support the work of the university.

BUILDING CAMPUSWIDE CONSENSUS AND SUPPORT FOR THE INFORMATION TECHNOLOGY (IT) VISION

The process of visioning and strategic planning requires tremendous emotional and physical energy, an openness to change, and an attitude predisposed to enjoying the experience. Aleister Crowley said that "The joy of life consists in the exercise of one's energies, continual growth, constant change, the enjoyment of every new experience. To stop means simply to die. The eternal mistake of mankind is to set up an attainable ideal" (Crowley, 1989: 602). This thoughtful quotation relates well to the work and desired outcomes of strategic planning and to the daily challenges faced by IT leadership and departments. The outcomes of a successful planning initiative should be an alignment of goals across organizational divisions, improved communication, and a heightened sense of community in which each person understands the institution's goals. This alignment helps to direct the uses of IT resources and better focus the growing demand from all organizational areas for IT support and expansion.

Strategic planning and visioning is essentially about communication and building consensus among people, departments, and the many constituencies of the institution. Rarely does this process take place in an environment that is not rich with history and records of past goals, reports, and evaluations. Through identification and discussion of commonly held values, review and synthesis of past reports and studies, a thorough assessment of the internal and external environment, and the drafting of a plan that reflects a consensus of the institution's most central values and goals, a strategic plan emerges. The document that is produced from the process should contain a number of lofty but addressable goals. They should be goals that individual departments and groups can use to develop implementation plans but goals that will never be completely fulfilled or attained. Ideally, the vision and broad goals remain relatively constant while the implementation plans developed at the division and department level change to meet the changing environment and evolving education and service delivery needs.

The task of building a campus-wide vision for IT must fundamentally be one of developing consensus. This can only be achieved where there is a level of trust established between the IT leadership and the various campus constituencies. This trust is founded upon good communication within the campus concerning IT issues, concerns, and developments, the existence of a true service attitude toward the delivery of technical support and services, and a history of acting in a collaborative manner concerning decisions that impact users and their information technology choices.

LEADERSHIP THROUGH COLLABORATION: A NEW STYLE OF IT LEADERSHIP

No aspect of higher education has experienced more change over the past 25 years than that of information technology. Hawkins and Battin described the dynamics of technological change in academe:

> "The initial incremental nature of technological change encouraged the widespread belief that the new technologies could be easily integrated into the existing management systems. As a result, the discontinuous revolutionary potential of digital technology and its implications for wrenching changes in enshrined assumptions have been widely ignored, misunderstood, and feared." (Hawkins and Battin, 1998: 6)

Billy Frye (2002) observed that information technology is exerting pressure on the academy to change by:

- changing the ways in which information is generated, evaluated, organized, preserved, and disseminated;
- rendering obsolete the traditional disciplinary boundaries of the academy's organization;
- finding radically new ways of creating, organizing, authenticating, accessing, and disseminating knowledge;
- credentialing those who discover and teach.

Computer technology has infiltrated nearly every facet of campus life and has frequently been employed as a change agent. But with all of the change that technological implementation has brought academic and administrative departments on the campus, no single department's role has been more impacted than that of the central Information Technology Service itself. The programmatic convergence of IT and library services due to digital technology promises to bring about even greater change in the future. On campuses today, the IT department is no longer the single campus "expert" with the knowledge to make technology decisions unilaterally. Today's campuses generally include many "pockets" of technology with their own "experts" within the library and academic and administrative departments. These experts generally have knowledge of the technologies specific to their disciplines and take ownership of determining which technology solutions they will employ, supporting that technology (to a point), and planning the future of technology in their areas. IT leaders must work collaboratively with these people to ensure that solutions adapt and integrate into the larger campus network environment. Responsibility for the

IT on a campus must be shared among all of the constituents—faculty, students, staff, departments, colleges—in part because no one unit is large and diverse enough to provide all things to all people or to determine priorities unilaterally in a resource-constrained system. The people who use technology generally feel best served when they can obtain IT support from someone who understands their "local" programmatic needs.

IT leaders must provide a new kind of leadership style that is much more collaborative than authoritative. This new leader is not the crusader who unilaterally determines "the answer" and sells the campus on particular technological solutions but rather is a facilitator who listens to many campus constituencies, encourages involvement and ownership of technological tools and processes, synthesizes the many needs and ideas, and articulates the collective IT vision for the campus.

PLANNING RESOURCES REQUIRED FOR USE OF TECHNOLOGY IN TEACHING AND LEARNING

A danger of strategic planning relative to IT is the tendency to be too specific in naming the technology solutions that will be employed. Given the rapid advancements in technology, strategic plans should address the desired outcomes rather than specific technologies employed to help achieve them. The implementation plans then detail how strategic goals will be addressed, name specific solutions, and are updated as needed over time. This ensures that the institution's strategic plan will not have to be revised each time a change in vendor or technological solution is implemented.

Typically, the range of resources that are needed for implementation of programs and support services identified in the broad strategic goals resulting from the strategic planning process are far beyond the resources available to the IT department. For the campus that prioritizes expanded access to education through online delivery, the services that must be developed or improved include

Internet bandwidth and quality of service (QOS) planning;
campus infrastructure that can carry multimedia and higher traffic;

computing support for 24/7 operation of central services such as electronic mail, online courseware, Web, and help desk;
resources to support faculty in developing and delivering online educational materials.

If academic departments plan new programs that create additional student enrollments or shift enrollments to online resources, a portion of tuition should be allocated for providing IT resources. IT leadership must participate in academic and administrative department discussions of services to ensure that hidden costs such as Internet bandwidth and campus infrastructure are not omitted in the planning of resources required to fulfill the plan. Most IT departments have been struggling to absorb increased campus use of information technology and computers without significant increases in human resources, space, or budget. To ensure success of institutional strategies that involve IT resources, organizations must plan for the expansion of services and support.

CONCLUSION: PEOPLE MAKE THE DIFFERENCE, AND TECHNOLOGY CAN HELP

In the final analysis, it is people who make the difference, and it is up to the IT leadership to listen, encourage, coach, and foster ongoing dialogue with all constituencies, describe the range of possible implementation strategies, articulate the campus vision and plan, and make final implementation decisions based upon a combination of what people want and what will be technically feasible. The best technological solutions are those that have "buy in" from the people who use and support them. Without substantial support and consensus from campus constituents, true success is not within the realm of possibility.

REFERENCES

Crowley, Aleister. 1989. *The Confessions of Aleister Crowley*. London: Penguin Books.

DeBard, Robert and Peck, Kelli D. 2000. "Moving from Oversight to Insight." *Planning for Higher Education* 28, no. 4 (Summer): 1–9.

Frye, E. 2002. Reflections. *EDUCAUSE Review* (January/February): 8–14.

Harvey, Bryan C. 1998. "The Perils of Planning before You Are Ready." *Planning for Higher Education* 26, no. 4 (Summer): 1–9.

Hawkins, Brian L. and Patricia Battin. 1998. *The Mirage of Continuity: Reconfiguring Academic Information Resources for the 21st Century.* Washington, D.C.: Council on Library and Information Resources and AAU.

Korschgen, Ann J., R. Fuller, and L. Lambert. 2000. "Institutional Planning That Makes a Difference." *AAHE Bulletin* (April): 7–10.

Rowley, Daniel James, Herman D. Lujan, and Michael G. Dolence. 1997. *Strategic Change in Colleges and Universities.* San Francisco: Jossey-Bass.

Yamada, M. M. 1991. *Joint Big Decision Committees and University Governance. New Directions for Higher Education,* ed. R. Birnbaum, no. 52. San Francisco: Jossey-Bass.

Chapter 2

Designing IT Strategic Planning for the Smaller Institution

C. Patrick Kohrman II
Chief Information Officer, Berks-Lehigh College, Pennsylvania State University

and

Dennis Trinkle
Associate Coordinator of Information Services and Technology and Tenzer Family University Professor in Instructional Technology, DePauw University

INTRODUCTION

For many smaller institutions the daily challenges of managing and leading an IT organization make strategic planning seem a luxury, an extravagance that only schools with far larger resources can afford. This attitude may be easy to understand, but it cannot be allowed to endure. Demands on IT organizations have never been greater, the pace of change has never been faster, and the stakes have never been higher. No IT organization, including the smaller IT organizations (and perhaps especially the smaller organizations), can afford the luxury of not being actively engaged in strategic planning. Failure to plan strategically condemns the IT department to a perpetual cycle of reaction and infrequent, incremental progress. Reactive crisis management never provides an Archimedean lever than can move an organization forward. Smaller organizations need an approach to strategic planning that recognizes their unique circumstances and resource limitations. The purpose of this article is to provide such a scalable strategic planning model.

THE WHAT AND WHY OF STRATEGIC PLANNING

Before discussing the process of strategic planning, it is appropriate to review what strategic planning is and why IT organizations should be engaged in strategic planning. First, what is strategic planning? Quite simply, strategic planning is a leadership and management tool. Bryson states, "As with any management tool, it is used for one purpose only: to help an organization do a better job—to focus its energy, to ensure that members of the organization are working toward the same goals, to assess and adjust the organization's direction in response to a changing environment. In short, strategic planning is a disciplined effort to produce fundamental decisions and actions that shape and guide what an organization is, what it does, and why it does it, with a focus on the future" (Bryson, 1995). Stated simply, strategic planning is a process for setting goals that align with an institution's mission and objectives and a process for guiding progress toward those goals.

Strategic planning is not about carving the Ten Commandments in stone for an organization. It is about creating a clear, compelling, achievable direction for the next one to five years and being prepared to adapt plans as changing circumstances require. While leading the Allied Forces during the Second World War, General Dwight D. Eisenhower remarked, "Plans are nothing. Planning is everything." It is the planning process that is most important. Planning is hard work and requires flexibility and commitment, but planning aligns the IT organization's goals with the college's goals, planning leads to sound management, planning translates visionary leadership into action, and planning builds credibility and support with all your stakeholders.

PLANNING BASICS

Strategic planning has five basic elements. These elements will serve as the road map for this chapter:

1. Vision and mission. Where do you want to go?
2. Assessment. Where are you now?
3. Strategic planning. What do we have to do to close the gap in the long term (three to five years)?
4. Tactical planning. What do we have to do to close the gap in the short term (less than one to two years)?
5. Integration and communication. How do we institutionalize the planning process at our campuses?

Vision and mission: Creating a strategic mission and vision for your organization

Albert Einstein said, "Problems that are created by our current level of thinking can't be solved by that same level of thinking." If leaders are to create successfully a strategic vision and mission for their organizations, they must think, plan, and operate at a new and different level. The strategic planning process can be an effective tool to help leaders think and act differently. More to the point, leaders must think differently if they are to create effective missions and visions for their organizations.

The first question to be addressed is "How should leaders think in relation to their organizational needs, challenges, and problems?" Answer: They must think and act strategically. In the next few pages we will explore an approach to strategic thinking and planning that may be useful to those leading information technology functions within educational institutions.

Stephen Haines suggests a five-phase planning model that invites the leader to ask and answer five important questions (Haines, 2000: 43–44).

- Where do we want to be?—Define your mission and vision.
- How will we know when we get there?—Determine your expected outcomes.
- Where are we now?—Perform an internal assessment.

- How do we get there from here?—Develop plans and actions for closing the gap.
- What is happening in the environment?—Monitor the external environment.

Asking and answering these questions initiates a process that can continue throughout the life of the organization and provides a means for continual evaluation and course correction. The process begins by asking the future-oriented question, "Where do we want to be?" This question requires the leader and the organization to articulate clearly the organization's mission and vision. The organization's mission statement should verbalize the organization's reason for existence. Peter Drucker reminded us "A business is not defined by the company's name, statutes, or articles of incorporation. It is defined by the want the customer satisfies when he buys a product or a service. To satisfy the customer is the mission and purpose of every business. The question 'What is our business?' can, therefore, be answered only by looking at the business from the outside, from the point of view of customer and market" (Drucker, 1974: 44). Within the educational institution the information technology function must be able to recognize its clients and identify their needs and wants accurately.

Who are the clients of the information technology function? A partial answer to that question could include students, faculty, administrators, alumni, supporters, parents of students, and other staff members. Once the needs and wants of each of these constituencies have been identified, a strategic statement of purpose, a mission statement, can be crafted. What would an effective mission statement look like? One example familiar to many is the following:

> We the People of the United States, in Order to form a more perfect Union, establish Justice, insure domestic Tranquility, provide for the common defense, promote the general Welfare, and secure the Blessings of Liberty to ourselves and our Posterity, do ordain and establish this Constitution for the United States of America. (The United States Constitution)

Examination of this profound mission statement reveals that it focuses on benefits; that is, a more perfect Union, Justice, domestic Tranquility, common defense, general Welfare, the Blessings of Liberty. When leaders craft an effective mission statement, it will focus on client benefits.

Examples of IT related mission statements include the following:

IT Unit, Berks-Lehigh Valley College, Penn State University	We are dedicated to providing superior service and innovative ideas to all our customers through effective communication and teamwork.
Information Services, DePauw University	We are here to support those living, learning, and working in the DePauw University community through emerging technologies. Our team provides innovative solutions, training, support, and leadership. We have the responsibility of maintaining and enhancing the technologies of today, while collaboratively envisioning the needs and opportunities of tomorrow.
IT Unit, George Mason University	The mission of the ITU organization is to advance the University's strategic goals, support learning, enable scholarly endeavors, and improve institutional management by effectively leveraging the information and technology resources of the ITU's constituent units. (George Mason University, 2002)
Information Systems, Wake Forest University	The Information Systems (IS) staff is committed to attaining the highest level of quality and integrity in all relationships with its clients. IS is dedicated to continually improving the services we provide to students, faculty and staff, through effective

	implementation and management of information technology products, services, and support. (Wake Forest University, 2002)
Academic Technology Center, Bentley College	The mission of Bentley's Academic Technology Center is to research, develop, and integrate technology into the curriculum that improves the teaching and learning process and prepares Bentley students to become business leaders in the information age. (Bentley College, 2002)

The mission statement is only one of the statements or documents used to provide direction for the organization. The organization, its leaders, and its constituents must also have a shared vision of where the organization is going in the future. The vision statement is an articulation of what the organization will become or where it will be in the future. Michael Mische (Mische, 1995) has suggested that the visioning process is a leadership function and that the organization's vision can become the rallying point for the organization. Not only must the vision statement be clearly articulated, it must be championed throughout the organization. In order for the vision statement to be an effective rallying point for the organization, all members of the organization should claim ownership of that vision. The information technology leader should be the champion of that vision. The champion must take every opportunity to promote the vision within the organization and also represent that vision to the clients of the organization. When a vision statement is crafted for the IT function, it must reflect in some way the vision for the institution. A possible IT vision statement may look like the following: "The vision for the Information Technology function is to be on the leading edge of technology developments and deliver appropriate technologies and services that support the mission and vision of the institution." The strength of the vision statement is based on its close connection to the institution's vision and mission and also the effectiveness with which it is articulated.

Orit Gadiesh and James L. Gilbert (Gadiesh and Gilbert, 2001) have proposed an approach to articulating an organization's mission and vision through the use of a strategic principle. A strategic principle is a distillation of the organization's mission and vision statements into a concise statement of direction and purpose. The function and purpose of the strategic principle is to provide direction for the members of the organization and to enable them to act quickly and strategically. When clearly stated, the strategic principle will enable members of the organization to make decisions and to act in harmony with the unit's strategic mission and vision.

Gadiesh and Gilbert propose three criteria for an "effective strategic principle":

1. It forces trade-offs between competing resource demands.
2. It tests the strategic soundness of a particular action.
3. It sets clear boundaries within which employees must operate while granting them freedom to experiment within those constraints (Gadiesh and Gilbert, 2001: 75).

Some examples of effective strategic principles provided by Gadiesh and Gilbert (2001: 74) include the following:

General Electric	Be number one or number two in every industry we compete with, or get out
Wal-Mart	Low prices, every day

Below are examples of strategic principles that could be used for the IT function (Kohrman, Renaud, and Trinkle, 2001):

Superior service, innovative ideas

Technology leadership, service, and innovation

Empowering clients through application of appropriate technology

Focused on learning

Gadiesh and Gilbert (2001: 78–79) propose a process for creating and evaluating a strategic principle that can serve as an effective rallying point and compass for the organization. Leaders should answer the following questions:

1. How do we allocate resources to create value in a unique way?
2. How do we differentiate ourselves from the competition?
3. Can we summarize the answers to the previous questions in a concise statement?
4. Does the statement address our core competencies?
5. Can the statement be articulated clearly, powerfully, and concisely?
6. Does it guide and promote appropriate action?
7. Does it force decision-making?

Answers to these questions should lead to the formation of a strategic principle that will motivate members of the organization and also provide clear direction on how to act. Once an effective strategic principle has been developed, it is the responsibility of the leader(s) to promote the principle internally and externally.

Effective mission statements, vision statements, and strategic principles will provide a long-range vision for the use of technology within the organization. They will also serve as a blueprint for ensuring that technology supports organizational goals and optimizes resources (Mische, 1995). It is also important to remember that information technology planning takes place within the framework of the institution. "Part of effective IT strategic planning in higher education is to remember that the top goals of any IT plan must be to support the top goals of the institution's strategic plan. The most important factors are leadership, shared institutional vision, and sustained communication" (Barone et al., 2000: 3).

Assessment: Before, during, and after strategic planning

Strategic planning is often viewed as being a sequential set of activities that starts with developing mission and vision statements. After articulation of the direction statements, planners then conduct assessment, perform gap analysis, set goals, and then develop plans to close the perceived gaps. The strategic planning process is not a purely sequential process. Instead, it is a process in which many activities occur concurrently. For institutions and their IT organizations to remain viable, assessment must be conducted continuously. In particular, assessment must be performed before, during, and after the visioning, goal setting, and planning occur.

Mission and vision statements serve to answer the question, "Where do we want to be?" (Haines, 2000: 43–44). Assessment can and should answer the following questions:

- How will we know when we get there?
- Where are we now?
- What is happening in the environment?

Susan B. Miller of the University of Wisconsin-Madison offers an assessment model that can be applied to the IT organization. She proposes that "Evaluation and assessment entail the following processes:

- Articulation of goals
- Specification of strategy
- Agreement on evidence of goal achievement
- Gathering, interpreting, and using the information" (Miller, 2001: 11)

Adoption of an assessment model such as that proposed by Miller can enable the IT organization to conduct its assessment and provide answers to the questions listed above. Before engaging in assessment, it is helpful to understand the purposes of the assessment process. Richard N. Katz and Julia A. Rudy have stated, "As information technologies enable new modes of instructional delivery, faculty roles and faculty relationships to students, technologists, and others will likely change in significant ways. . . . The failure to anticipate new information requirements, to develop the information systems that support such requirements, and to acquire and manage the new information will put traditional institutions at a serious disadvantage in competitive markets . . ." (1999: 3). In addition, Taylor and Eustis suggest two purposes for assessment: feedback and communication (Katz and Rudy, 1999: 64). According to Taylor and Eustis, feedback is designed to provide information to those directly involved in projects or functions being assessed. The feedback should be provided in a timely fashion to allow for course corrections as needed. From this perspective, feedback becomes a management tool used to provide direction and management of a project or function. Taylor and Eustis describe communication as a tool for presenting results of completed projects or activities to the project or departmental stakeholders. Communication focuses on such concepts as "What were the outcomes? Was the project successful? What groups or individuals were impacted? Are the results replicable?" These purposes must be kept in mind as decisions are made regarding what to assess and how to conduct the assessment activities.

Susan J. Foster and David E. Hollowell ask a pertinent question with regard to assessment and also provide an answer (Katz and Rudy, 1999: 10). The question: "What are the relevant attributes that must be known in order to achieve effective IT planning and develop information technologies strategically?" The answer:

- Who is using the information or service?
- Who is providing the information or service?
- What is the nature of the information or service?
- What outcomes or benefits are expected?
- Will the resources meet demand?
- Are the resources and services reliable and supportable?
- Can the resources sustain growth?

Examination of the preceding questions provides some focus for the types of questions that might be asked in the assessment process, but what should be assessed? Within the educational institution, learning outcomes should be identified and assessed, as should impact on performance of administrative staff, support staff, and faculty; impact on students; impact on services; and impact on other stakeholders. Assessment should focus on what is done, how it is done, how well it is done, and what outcomes are being realized. When viewed from this perspective, assessment appears to be a daunting task and rightly so. Each organization must find an approach to conducting the assessment process that will fit its budgets, manpower, organizational culture, and goals.

How should assessment be conducted? Simple answer: Ask questions. However, the process used for asking those questions may not be so simple. That process can be as rigorous as the budget can afford. It does not need to be expensive to provide useful information. The key is to ask questions. It may be useful to keep in mind the following guidelines when asking questions: (1) the questions should focus on how well the IT function is achieving its stated mission, vision, and goals; (2) questions should be asked of all constituencies—faculty, students, staff, administrators, and external stakeholders; and (3) evaluative comments should be sought from peers at other institutions.

One of the most persistent questions in the strategic planning and assessment process is who should conduct the assessment. If you are responsible for strategic planning for the IT function, you are responsible for the assessment of IT. Self-assessment is an effective place to begin the assessment process. Stephen G. Haines (Haines, 2000: 173) proposed a self-assess-

1. Are employees able to access computer and telephone networks from remote locations?
   ❑ Yes ❑ No ❑ Not Sure
2. Do all employees share a common software platform?
   ❑ Yes ❑ No ❑ Not Sure
3. Can your customers place orders with you electronically?
   ❑ Yes ❑ No ❑ Not Sure
4. Is the primary form of internal communications electronic (e-mail,bulletin boards, voice mail)?
   ❑ Yes ❑ No ❑ Not Sure
5. Do most of your workstations have processors the equivalent of Pentium® or better?
   ❑ Yes ❑ No ❑ Not Sure
6. Does your company use "distance learning" to educate its employees?
   ❑ Yes ❑ No ❑ Not Sure

7. Does your company have a technology manager who is part of its top management team?

   ❑ Yes ❑ No ❑ Not Sure

8. Can your employees run software applications when the network is down?

   ❑ Yes ❑ No ❑ Not Sure

ment tool that was produced by Arthur Andersen and is presented below:

With only small modifications this instrument could easily be adapted for educational institutions. For example, replace the word "company" with the word "institution." The term "employees" might be broadened to include students, faculty, and staff. Question three could be re-worded to read, "Can your students, staff, and faculty conduct business through institutional intranets and Web sites?" Answers to these questions will prepare the planner to ask further questions in the assessment process.

Assessment will and should involve asking questions of both internal and external constituencies. Questions asked of internal groups should include these: Are we meeting your current needs? How can we better serve you? What are your future needs or plans? Questions asked of external groups should include these: What are the trends in the field of higher education? How do we compare to other institutions? What potential threats exist? What potential opportunities exist?

There is a wide array of approaches to asking questions. Some methodologies are very structured and formal in their design; others are less formal in design and implementation. Your choice of methodology will be influenced by time, budget, and cultural constraints. Some of the more formal methods that could be considered are the following:

- Heiralliance Evaluation Guidelines for Institutional Information Resources (2000). This is an excellent resource provided by the Association of Research Libraries, CAUSE, and Educom. It is available at little or no cost and provides a structured approach to conducting an assessment of the IT function.

- Flashlight Project (www.tltgroup.org). This is a well-known group that provides a mature set of products for institutions to conduct assessment.
- Past strategic plans can be taken off the shelf (where unfortunately many are often found) and reviewed.
- If your institution has participated in accreditation reviews, the reports of the accrediting agencies can provide useful information for the assessment and planning process.
- Benchmarking studies can provide useful information for the assessment process. The Educause Effective Practices and Solutions Web site can be a useful starting point for these benchmarking studies.

Less formal techniques can also provide useful information for the strategic planning process. Below are some effective techniques:

- Bagels with Vince. Vince Sheehan, Director of University Information Systems at IUPUI, shared his approach. On a weekly basis he invites selected individuals to meet with him for bagels, coffee, and a chat. This method has allowed him to keep in touch with the individuals his department supports on an ongoing basis.
- Informal personal interviews, small focus group meetings, or some other version of Bagels with Vince.
- Short, targeted surveys to faculty, staff, or students. These surveys can be administered as hard-copy surveys or even by e-mail or via the institution's Web site. An example of a simple tool available for creating online surveys is Zoomerang (2002). This and other similar tools facilitate survey creation, administration, data collection, and reporting of results.

Regardless of the assessment tools employed, it ultimately becomes incumbent on leaders to use the information distilled through the assessment process. Leaders must incorporate the results of the assessment process into the strategic plan and then translate the plan into effective actions that enable the institution to fulfill its mission and vision. Joel Barker, President of Infinity, Ltd. (Watson, 1993: xiv) stated it well:

> "Vision without action is just a dream.
> Action without vision is just activity.
> Vision and action together can change the world."

For the strategic planning process not to be a futile effort, plans must incorporate the results of assessment, and plans must be translated into effective actions.

From vision to action: Setting strategic goals and objectives

Once a small institution has outlined and defined its overall mission and vision, the next step is to assess and specify the specific goals and objectives that will translate this vision into concrete steps. It is very helpful in planning to break these concrete deliverables into long-term goals (three to five years) and short-term objectives. The terms "goals" and "objectives" here are not important. The key point is to think in terms of long-term, more flexible action items, and short-term, more fixed action items. These short-term objectives ultimately will be associated with specific staff roles, time lines, and budgets.

In sum, to move from vision to action, you will:

- Establish long-term goals (three to five years)
- Establish strategies to reach goals
- Establish specific, measurable objectives (up to one year) to achieve those goals
- Associate responsibilities and time lines with each objective

Establish goals: A set of guidelines for creating departmental or team level objectives

There are many approaches to setting goals that work in a small institution. Some colleagues gather for a one-day retreat with a whiteboard and Post-it Notes, then they proceed to write down all the specific goals that they believe ought to be achieved in support of their vision and post them on the whiteboards. They spend the remainder of the day organizing and prioritizing these goals, and at the end they have, in the span of a single day, arrived at their goals. This is certainly an effective and lean approach that a department with limited time and resources can employ effectively. Below is a broader process for setting goals. This process is no more fixed than an Eisenhower plan. However, it can be modified to meet a smaller institution's particular characteristics:

A model for goal setting

- Departmental Groups review and discuss the goal-setting process and its place in the overall strategic planning process.
- Departmental Groups review topics on the Watch List. Distribution of this information will set the stage for formulating goals.
- The Leadership Team sets direction from these conversations to achieve desired results.
- Determine if the organization is headed in the right direction or if minor or major changes will be necessary.
- The Leadership Team drafts and refines goals:
    - ◊ Review goals developed previously and revise as appropriate
    - ◊ Determine if the goals are feasible-link to budget planning
    - ◊ Consider the factors or conditions that will facilitate or hinder goal achievement
    - ◊ Foster consensus among all participants on the goal statements and be committed to the completion of the goals.

Departmental organization varies and will effect the above scheme. The model above presumes that an IT department is divided into sub-teams such as Network Operations or Academic Computing. Some organizations will prefer to have these groups meet individually first, then gather to set department goals collectively. Others will prefer to have the senior departmental leaders generate a synthesis from the work of the departmental groups and report back. Either way, departmental groups must clearly understand what is expected of them in the goal creation process and must also understand and accept the goal criteria. Below are some suggested criteria or guidelines that can be used when establishing goals.

Criteria for goals

- Goals are in harmony with vision, mission, and principles.
- Goals clarify the mission of the organization.
- Achievement of the goals will fulfill or help fulfill the mission of the organization.
- Goals represent a desired *result* and lead to development of performance measures and longer range performance targets.
- Goals chart a *clear* direction for the organization but will not determine specific ways to get there.
- Goals encompass a relatively long period—at least three years or more. If a goal can be accomplished in less than three years, it is probably an objective.
- Goals do not set specific milestones or determine how to accomplish goals. Objectives and strategies or action plans will do that.
- Goals tend to remain essentially unchanged until a shift in the environment under which they were created occurs.
- Goals do not conflict with each other.
- Goals are challenging but realistic and achievable.

The goal setting process really reduces to a simple question: What should the institution or IT organization do over the next three to five years to advance the institution and pursue the institution's strategic mission and vision? A matrix developed by Fred Nickles can be used to plot all the possibilities. This matrix provides a visual method for evaluating the importance and desirability of all goals in concrete and specific terms.

Objectives

Selecting and defining goals leads to the next stage in the strategic planning process. The next stage is to break the goals down

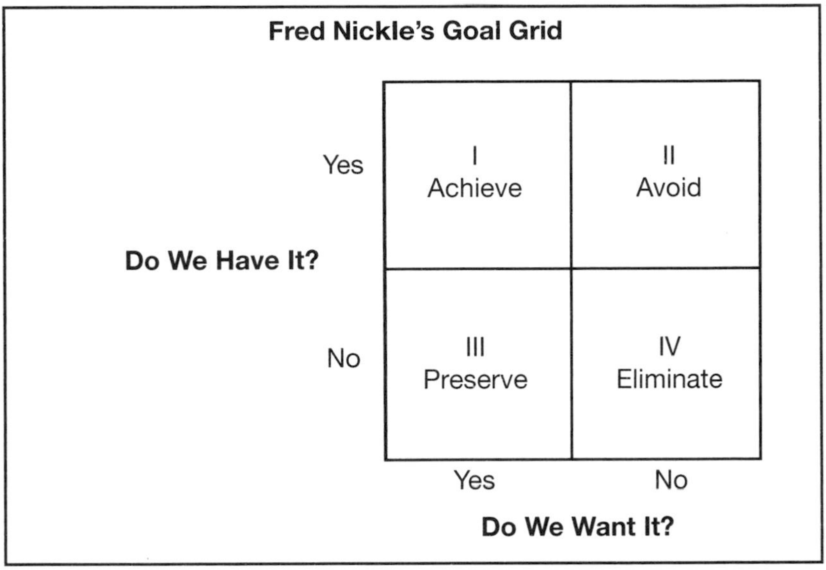

into their component short-term objectives. At one small institution, our colleague Robert Renaud has the leadership team and the various departments define objectives related to each goal. These short-term objectives are the action points where the rubber meets the road. Each objective should be a specific target designed to achieve a particular program goal. In contrast to goals (which are broad, general statements of long-range purposes), objectives are specific, quantifiable, and time-bound statements of a desired accomplishment or result.

To create effective objectives, it is useful to remember a simply acronym: SMART. A SMART goal or objective is:

Specific
Measurable
Aggressive but attainable
Rewarding
Time-bound

Specific

Objectives should reflect specific accomplishments that are desired, not ways to accomplish them. The objectives should be clearly and precisely defined. It is difficult to know what someone should be doing if they are to pursue the goal to "work harder." It's easier to understand and achieve "Get all new faculty computers installed by September 15."

Measurable

An objective must be measurable to determine when it has been accomplished. Accountability and measurable criteria for goals should be built into the planning process. As Edward Deming, an international leader in the field of total quality management, used to assert, you cannot manage what you cannot measure. It is hard to assess success with a goal such as "Improve customer satisfaction." Conversely, an objective such as "Raise customer 'very satisfied' responses to 65% on customer surveys." has built into it a method for measuring whether the goal has been achieved.

Aggressive but attainable

If objectives are to be standards for achievement, they should challenge but should not demand the impossible. Objectives should be realistic and attainable. It is important, therefore, not to define more objectives than can realistically be attained. Fewer focused and meaningful objectives are much better than a large number of poorly defined ones. Even if you do accept responsibility to achieve an objective that is specific and measurable, the goal will not be useful if it is unrealistic and unachievable. Goals such as "Improve customer satisfaction to 110% within one year" are ineffective.

Rewarding

Individuals push harder to achieve goals and objectives when they can clearly see the benefit to themselves and the organization.

Time-bound

Specify a time frame for meeting objectives. Each objective

should be attainable within a relatively short time period: from a few weeks to no more than a year. If an objective runs over such a specific time period, it may be operational in nature and not be a candidate for an objective. If an objective legitimately spans more than one fiscal year, it should normally be broken down into annual phases.

A SMART Planning Template

Strategic Goal	Strategy	Objective	Responsibility	Time Line
1. (Goal #1)	1.1 (first strategy to reach Goal #1)	1.1.1 (first objective to reach while implementing Strategy #1.1)	(who's going to accomplish that objective)	(when the implementer is going to be accomp-lishing that objective)

To conserve scarce time and resources and set SMART objectives, follow this simple process:

- Review the goals within the team.
- Decide what key results are wanted. Bearing in mind that operational work consumes the bulk of a team's time, limit objectives to those key, high payoff efforts that move the college and department forward.
- Set a time frame for achieving results.
- Build in accountability.

Cycling through this process and breaking each goal into objectives will flesh out the strategic plan objective by objective.

This table illustrates a poor objective.

A Poor Sample Objective

Team	Description	Related to IS Goal	Owner	Activities and Time Line
Frontline Team	Begin to think about replacing the ABC Booking System.	2.3	Frontline Team	By the end of the next academic year.

This table illustrates a good objective.

A Good Sample Objective

Team	Description	Related to IS Goal	Owner	Activities and Time Line
Frontline Team	Analyze alternatives to ABC Booking System, report to Leadership Team, and create budget submission for full-year cycle.	2.3 2.7	Jane Smith	Review existing functionality (7/2000) Gather information on comparable products (8/2000) Define comparative criteria (9/2000) Rank and cost alternatives (10/2000) Bring report to LT (11/2000) Package recommendation for budget process (12/2000)

This table provides an example of a good departmental or team level objective.

A Good Departmental or Team Level Objective

Objective Number and Description	Related to IS Goal	Owner	Activities, Time line, Justification
Technical Support: System and Equipment	2	Martha Berry	May 2001: Advertise Position
Technician for Academic	3		June 2001: Interview Candidates
Departmental Computer labs	4		July 2001: Select Candidate and Offer Position August 2001: Position filled Currently, IS does not support departmental computer labs. Departmental faculty and staff maintain their own computer labs and provide system administration. However, faculty assignments are being shifted so many of the labs will not have technical support after June 2001. IS has one computer lab position and it is not fea- sible to have one person cover both IS labs, the courseware servers and also service the departmental labs. This request is for a full- time position to provide technical support and system administration for the academic departments' computer labs.

INTEGRATION

After defining the strategic mission, vision, goals, and objectives, the final element of the strategic planning process is integration. This synergistic phase links the IT organization's mission, vision, goals, and objectives to the institution's mission, vision, goals, and objectives and to institutional and departmental budget processes, and clarifies how performance evaluations will be tied to the plan and the planning process. For the plan and the planning process to succeed, the integration step is vital. Countless well-crafted strategic plans have become ornamental bookends because they were not integrated into the institutional process.

To guarantee that the plan is implemented, be sure to address each of the following steps:

- review the goals within the team;
- set a time frame for achieving results;
- build in accountability—link objectives directly to performance reviews;
- link objectives to the budget planning process.

Here is one model for linking the strategic planning process to the budget cycle:

Information Sharing	**Start**	**End**	**Responsible**
Conduct IS futures sessions	Jun	Jul	Leadership Team
IS Dept. annual report	Aug	Sep	Leadership Team
Annual planning cycle	**Start**	**End**	**Responsible**
Review Watch List and revise	May	Jun	Leadership Team
Prepare white papers on selected Watch List topics	Jun	Jul	
Review IS goals relative to overall university strategy	Aug	Aug	Leadership Team
Develop and cost objectives, Round 1	Sep	Sep	Teams

Review goals and draft objectives	Oct	Oct	Leadership Team IS Committee
Develop and cost objectives, Round 2	Oct	Oct	Teams
Review and comment	Nov	Nov	IS Committee Campus Community
Develop and cost objectives, Final Round	Nov	Dec	Leadership Team
Revise annual plan and post to Web	Jan	Jan	Leadership Team
Budget Planning Cycle	**Start**	**End**	**Responsible**
Package operating budget request for Finance	Dec	Dec	Leadership Team Budget Assistant

360 DEGREE COMMUNICATION: KEYSTONE TO PLANNING AND INTEGRATION

A final and key ingredient for successful integration and implementation of the mission, vision, and planning processes is effective 360 degree communication. For the planning process to succeed fully, campus IT leaders must communicate effectively upward and outward, as well as with the members of their staff. Many studies have demonstrated that the most common reason planning efforts fail is poor communication or undercommunication (Schwalbe, 2000: 242). For this reason, we recommend that IT leadership adopt a policy of overcommunication to all stakeholders. Overcommunication is especially important in the initial stages of planning and implementation. The goal of overcommunication is to ensure that not only do all the stakeholders hear the same message, but all the stakeholders have the same interpretation and understanding of the message—the message in this case being the mission, vision, and goals.

A primary aspect of overcommunication is getting out

among the stakeholders, listening to their views, and promoting the mission, vision, processes, and values. Some term this MBWO—management by walking around. It is more than that; it is also leadership by communication and presence.

Whether one literally or metaphorically walks around, some excellent suggestions for communicating full circle are offered by John Kotter in his recent book on leadership (1996: 90):

1. Keep it simple: Eliminate the jargon from your communications.
2. Use metaphors, analogies, stories, and examples: A verbal picture is worth more than a thousand words.
3. Use multiple forums: Use every meeting, big and small meetings, memos, company and departmental newspapers, and informal interactions for spreading the word.
4. Repeat, repeat, repeat: Repeat the message again and again and again.
5. Walk the talk: The old adage, "Actions speak louder than words," applies here. Make sure that your behavior is consistent with your message. Inconsistent behavior will scuttle your efforts.
6. Explain the inconsistencies: Address any apparent inconsistencies with clear, honest information.
7. Don't do all of the talking: You must also listen. Two-way communication is much more effective than one-way communication.

On a practical level, all communications need to be well-crafted and the actual content well-thought out. A simple communication matrix can be constructed and used to conduct a stakeholder analysis. Dimensions in the matrix might include: Who should know what and when? How often do key stakeholders need to be informed? What format do they prefer?

For the strategic planning process to be successful and effective, the communication process must be effective in both anticipating and responding to the informational needs of all constituencies. Most critically, communications must sharply identify the impact on the "bottom line" for all stakeholders. This bottom line will be financial, psychological, social, organization, cultural, or technological, depending upon the individual's perspective. IT leadership must recognize all these check points and be sure to anticipate and address them fully. For example, institutional management needs to know how the institution will be affected by the IT organization's mission, vision, and plans. Will more staff need to be hired? Will budgets need to be increased (or decreased)? Will funds need to be shifted from one area to another? Will fees need to be increased? How will services be improved? Will costs be lowered and by how much and over what time period? Employees within the department need to know how their work will be affected. Will some employees lose their jobs? Will re-training be required? Will salaries go up or down? How will the workload change? How will reporting lines be affected? How will interactions with clients, students, faculty, or staff change? These are just a sampling of the types of questions that will need to be answered throughout the planning process. The success of the organization's planning efforts will rise and fall on the back of the communication process.

CONCLUSION

The planning process is not designed to lock the IT organization into an inflexible pattern of operation. The planning process is designed to provide the IT organization with the flexibility to effectively respond to the changing needs of the institution and to the changing environment of that institution. It is worth repeating here two important quotes. First, Dwight D. Eisenhower stated, "Plans are nothing. Planning is everything." Planning is the instructive process that will prepare the organization to anticipate and respond to change. Second, Joel Barker, President of Infinity, Ltd., declared, "Vision and action together can change the world" (Watson, 1993). Planning, action, and communication together will serve as the Archimedean lever that can and will move the IT organization forward.

REFERENCES

Barone, Carole A., Robert F. German, Jr., Richard N. Katz, Philip E. Long, and Barry Walsh. 2000. *Information Technology, Systems, and Services in Higher Education: A Primer*. Educause and NACUBO.

Bentley College. 2002. [Online]. Available: *http://atc.bentley.edu*. [16 January 2002].

Bryson, John Moore. 1995. *Strategic Planning for Public and Nonprofit Organizations: A Guide to Strengthening and Sustaining Organizational Achievement*. San Francisco: Jossey-Bass.

Constitution of the United States of America

Drucker, Peter. 1974. *Management: Tasks, Responsibilities, Practices*. New York: Harper & Row.

Educause Effective Practices and Solutions. n.d. [Online]. Available: *www.educause.edu/ep/*. [21 January 2002].

Foster, Susan J. and David E. Hollowell. 1999. Integrating Information Technology Planning and Funding at the Institutional Level. In *Information Technology in Higher Education: Assessing Its Impact and Planning for the Future,* edited by Richard N. Katz and Julia A. Rudy. San Francisco: Jossey-Bass, 9–19.

Gadiesh, Orit and James L. Gilbert. 2001. "Transforming Corner-Office Strategy into Frontline Action." *Harvard Business Review* 79, no. 5 (May): 72–79.

George Mason University. 2002. [Online]. Available: *http://itu.gmu.edu/mission.shtml*. [16 January 2002].

Haines, Stephen G. 2000. *The Systems Thinking Approach to Strategic Planning and Management*. Boca Raton, Fla.: CRC Press.

Heiralliance Evaluation Guidelines for Institutional Information Resources. 2000. [Online]. Available: *www.educause.edu/collab/heirapapers/hei2000.html*. [18 January 2002].

Katz, Richard N. and Julia A. Rudy, eds. 1999. Integrating Information Technology Planning and Funding at the Institutional Level. *Information Technology in Higher Education: Assessing Its Impact and Planning for the Future*. San Francisco: Jossey-Bass.

Kohrman II, C. Patrick, Robert Renaud, and Dennis Trinkle. 2001. IT Strategic Planning for the Smaller Institution. Educause Pre-conference Workshop. Indianapolis.

Kotter, John P. 1996. *Leading Change*. Boston: Harvard Business School Press.

Miller, Susan B. 2001. "Lessons on Assessment and Evaluation from the LEAD Center." *Syllabus: New Dimensions in Education Technology* 14, no. 7 (February): 10–12.

Mische, Michael. 1995. "Transnational Architecture: A Reengineering Approach." *Information Systems Management* 12, no. 1(Winter): 17–25.

Schwalbe, Kathy. 2000. *Information Technology Project Management*. Cambridge, Mass.: Thomson Learning.

Taylor, C. David and Joanne D. Eustis. 1999. Assessing the Changing Impact of Technology on Teaching and Learning at Virginia Tech. In *Information Technology in Higher Education: Assessing Its Impact and Planning for the Future*, edited by Richard N. Katz and Julia A. Rudy. San Francisco: Jossey-Bass, 55–70.

TLT Group (Teaching, Learning, and Technology). Flashlight Program for the Study and Improvement of Education and Uses of Technology [Online]. Available: *www.tltgroup.org/programs/flashlight.htm*. [24 January 2002].

Wake Forest University. 2002. Wake Forest University Information Systems Mission Statement [Online]. Available: *www.wfu.edu/Computer-information/about_is/mission.htm*. [16 January 2002].

Watson, Gregory H. 1993. *Strategic Benchmarking: How to Rate Your Company's Performance against the World's Best*. New York: John Wiley & Sons.

Zoomerang. 2000. [Online]. Available: *http://zoomerang.com/*. [21 January 2002].

Chapter 3

Finding the Vision: Shaping Technology Support Services in the Twenty-First Century Institution

LOIS BROOKS
Director of Academic Computing, Stanford University

Innovations in technology have been profound, and their impact on higher education, while perhaps not profound, have certainly created new possibilities. Two changes in particular, personal computing and the Internet, have touched nearly every faculty, staff, and student in American higher education. Many of our schools have undertaken new initiatives that relate to technology: distance education, international teaching and learning partnerships, installations of emerging technology, and course support systems, all garnering major institutional investments and spawning new demands on central and distributed computing support organizations. By and large, instructional technology units have dramatically increased their efforts to respond responsibly to the challenges over the past two decades. Structured support models, such as help desks, training programs, and investment planning for technology, are the norm on most of our campuses. We seem to have made a great deal of progress, so why consider new models?

There are compelling reasons to shape a new framework for academic technology services—that is, the information technology (IT) services that support teaching and learning. As faculty and student demand for information technology grows, and as institutions embark on technology-based projects, IT organizations will increasingly be required to collaborate with the faculty and students to define and deploy new technology services and infrastructure. Implementing these technologies effectively and efficiently may well be more complex than incorporating enterprise-wide administrative systems (the IT services that support the business functions of the university), a process that has been expensive and challenging on many campuses. Technology has evolved to allow tremendous flexibility and capability for the individual. Computers and consumer electronics are more powerful and less costly than ever before, software tools are increasingly easy to use, and individuals are simultaneously connected and mobile. These trends are enabling the end user to exploit technology in learning, teaching, research, and individual academic exploration in new and innovative ways. The demand for new kinds of academically driven services like personal digital archives, collaboration technologies, and innovative learning spaces will permeate our campuses.

Academia's relationship with technology will change at an institutional level. Deployment of new technology will no longer be considered experimental. Academic institutions will expect emerging technology to be stable and usable and will expect new technology to integrate with other institutional systems and services. Increasingly, institutional leadership will expect technology-based initiatives like distance education and collaborative learning projects to function on existing infrastructure rather than requiring major technological upgrades. At the same time, since the amount of available content is exploding, campus infrastructure will have to be able to accommodate vast digital repositories of data that require new management and navigation tools.

Programmatic initiatives based on technology will become commonplace. Teaching and research programs will expect to exchange information digitally both within the campus and with colleagues around the world. Departments will build shared resources, like digital libraries of teaching materials, that can be browsed and shared by faculty. Community life will be enhanced by technology. Digital face books, computer-based discussion, and technology-rich community spaces are just a few ways that the residential experience will be touched.

Scholarly use of technology will change. Students and faculty will turn first to online resources for research and will expect depth of information, excellent guides and searching capabilities, and multimedia as well as text-based content. There will be rich resources of materials that can be personalized—for example, annotated—for use in teaching, learning, and research. Security of personal work and openness of information exchange will be expected. Personal digital publishing will be the most common way that faculty and students share their work. Faculty and students will develop collections of materials from multiple sources, annotate or otherwise personalize online content, and display their collections. They will expect their work to be supported "behind the scenes" by network-based technologies—storage, application services, and knowledgeable staff.

As universities move into new realms of academic uses of technology, they will expect new service models from technology support providers. Support organizations will be valued for the instructional achievements they make possible rather than for the difficulty of the tasks they have undertaken or for quantitative measures of efficiency like numbers of users or online classes. Effort alone will not be enough: the support organization of the future will be held accountable for contributing to effective programmatic achievement. The successful service organization will adapt to the changing initiatives in the academy and to particular and varied user needs and processes. IT leaders must be able to demonstrate and assure that resources are appropriately targeted.

Since universities continually evolve because of technology-based initiatives and programmatic changes, IT organizations must constantly adjust the content of their service and the way it is delivered to assure alignment with the priorities of the institution. For example, a shift toward project-based learning in undergraduate classes may signal a need for IT organizations to provide more collaborative study space, tools that support virtual collaboration and iteration of project materials, and better presentation tools and facilities for classes. Similarly, a new grant program for technology innovation in the humanities may signal a need for a support model that includes technology planning with grant recipients.

Even as service units adapt their models, they are charged with providing seamless and stable support for basic technology infrastructure—networks, computers, technology-enhanced facilities, distributed computing infrastructure, security, digital content—the list goes on. At the same time, the funding available for technology is not rising as quickly as the expectations for what will be available and how it will be supported, creating an increasingly wide resource gap.

Support organizations must respond to increasing and evolving expectations in the face of competition for funding. Changing priorities in the institution, expensive and visible initiatives, and increasing expectations for ubiquitous and seamless service create challenges for IT support organizations. We must reshape our services to fit the new paradigm.

A MANDATE FOR CHANGE

First and most fundamental, leaders in information technology must change their perspective of the service organization. In the 1980s and 1990s, while technology change was rampant outside the institution, within higher education many of the changes were driven by central IT organizations that had direct control over major technological resources. For example, these organizations systematically installed networks on campuses, rolled out administrative systems that forced new work practices, and in some schools, contributed to requiring the use of technology by faculty and students. Support strategies were developed to enable successful completion of these projects but did not always consider the unique needs of academic disciplines or the work styles of the scholar.

A new perspective that embraces academic initiatives and

that provides support structures for faculty and students will align with academic priorities. Information technology organizations will need to examine the way in which existing resources are managed. The bandwidth problems faced on many campuses today are an example of this issue. The use of bandwidth, particularly by students, has grown in ways unforeseen ten or fifteen years ago when networks were installed. Most of us did not predict the explosion of multimedia and peer-to-peer technologies that have allowed the possibility of exploiting existing network technologies beyond their capacity. And while we might have predicted the use of technology for collaboration around the world, the enthusiasm of faculty and students for collaboration and the availability of tools that easily allow video, voice, and data to be shared over networks have taxed our networks more than many imagined possible ten years ago.

Similarly, the use of technology in faculty and students' individual academic exploration might raise the need for investments that are beyond the traditional choices made for technology funding, for example, learning spaces in student residences. The choices made in allocating resources must reflect academic priorities. As IT organizations make decisions on behalf of the institution about how to respond to these and other issues, faculty and students will need to be partners in decision-making processes that assure that the resulting policies and practices value the teacher and learner while responsibly managing resources.

The central and distributed IT organization must align its contribution with the institution's needs while remaining attentive to the complex issues raised by the rapid rate of change of technology. A perspective that enables rather than disallows and that prioritizes the academic mission of the institution must permeate IT service organizations.

STRATEGIC INVESTMENTS

The dilemma presented by the increasing gap between expectations and funding requires careful choices about how to use the resources available for technology. Most IT units have developed tactical responses to the increasing volume of service requests: customized skill sets among help desk staff allow a relatively small staff to respond to a variety of requests; regular training programs help users adopt new technology; standardization (or at many schools, alluring pricing to promote homogeneous acquisition) helps to limit the number of different technologies help desk staff must support. Still, service organizations must scramble to keep up with the number of requests and make choices about limiting the ways they can be helpful in order to manage staff workloads.

Such resource challenges have encouraged more strategic thinking and planning. For example, course management systems offer faculty the possibility of deploying course materials and information without a steep technical learning curve. These systems have significant support requirements and costs but in general allow more faculty to supplement their classes with Web sites than otherwise might have done so and allow support staff to better optimize their knowledge and time. Course management systems have limitations as well, most notably that courses must fit within the bounds of the system to be supported, and courses that need technology beyond the lowest common denominator still request IT organizations to create boutique services. Nonetheless, course management systems are a first step toward a more strategic support model. They have given faculty and students a new instructional opportunity, while repositioning the potential offerings of the IT support organization through an investment in technology.

Service organizations can respond strategically to the expectations versus funding gap by increasing their upfront investments in technology that is enabling, supportable, and scalable. Following are just a few ways to make strategic investments in technology. Investments that allow technology to serve a variety of purposes and allow services to be extended without major customization will help to close the resource gap.

Develop infrastructure that has multiple uses. Investments in multipurpose technology, coupled with collaborative deployment, will make better use of resources and will improve service to faculty and students. Reusable technology underpinnings allow the delivery of a suite of services or technologies that meet a wider set of needs. For example, a commonly available set of course rosters can be used to enhance access to electronic reserves, to limit participation in electronic discussions to class members, to expedite online grade submission, and so on. Similarly, development of mechanisms to upgrade software versions and refresh computer images can be multipurposed throughout the institution. The same technology can be used to update public workstations in the libraries and campus computer clusters, as well as to update specialized computer installations located in campus departments. Automated deployment of software upgrades can allow users to take advantage of new technology without spending undue staff time on installing software on individual computers. By adopting multipurpose technology, support organizations can extend the ways the technology is used at much lower cost than if using many specialized technologies.

Regularly upgrade hardware and software. The cost of maintaining equipment that is years out of date, although often hidden, is too great to ignore. If equipment lingers into obsolescence, faculty and staff are unable to take advantage of digital resources. Repair costs escalate, and support staff are required to maintain knowledge of older systems and software. A regular hardware and software replacement cycle, deployed campus-wide, proves both cost-effective and enabling. Economies of scale can be achieved, and common and time-consuming problems of compatibility across systems are reduced.

Develop facilities that support multiple uses and complement user needs. It is sometimes possible to configure and use technology-based facilities such as classrooms and computer labs to suit multiple purposes. For example, computer classrooms might serve as computer clusters of individual workstations when classes are not in session. Specialized computer labs might be configured to host training sessions and to support student project teams. By using facilities in multiple ways, investments in technology can be reduced and staff time optimized.

STRATEGIC SUPPORT MODELS

Defining the structure of support is as important as making strategic choices in how to invest technology dollars. A strategic support model must closely align with the needs of the institution, is flexible enough to accommodate changing technology and priorities, and models services in ways that work for the user. There is no one right support model. Just as universities vary in academic programs, residential opportunities, athletic programs, and so on, service units vary widely as well. Articulating the goals of the service organization provides a focus for the services provided.

Defining what each IT organization does is important for several reasons. First, it allows a common message to be given to staff, clients, and the institution about what can be expected from the organization. This message is used in many different contexts, both within and outside of the organization: it is given to administrators when asking for resources or proposing new initiatives; to new students and faculty when they arrive on campus; to prospective employees; and to colleagues at other schools. A clear, consistent, and easily understood message allows every member of the organization to accurately represent what the organization does. Second, a guiding set of principles helps to keep the organization on track with the mission of the institution. When making choices about whether to deploy a new project or to redirect resources away from an existing service toward a new initiative, the decision-making process should include consideration of whether the outcome will be in focus with the purpose of the university or if it will pull the organization off track. If the broad goals of the organization are defined, the decision-making process can be attuned accordingly. Finally, defining the goals of the organization helps each staff member to understand how his or her job is relevant. For example, if the organizational goals include providing opportunities for student leadership, staff members will understand that engaging students in varied aspects of projects is important. If the organizational goals include expertise with technology, staff training and skill development opportunities will be recognized as important within the organization.

Defined goals should be broad and clearly understood and should articulate the purpose of the organization. They should help the organization find focus and balance and should be employed throughout the organization. These goals are especially important for large, central IT organizations that are responsible for a wide range of services.

Equally important is achieving balance within the organization. The pieces of the organization should align with the overall mission and should fit with each other. Organizational components that dilute focus on achieving the goals of the organization should be eliminated.

There are guiding principles that can help determine whether a service is well aligned or is out of alignment with the institution's core needs. When evaluating services, consider the uniqueness of each effort. Some services should be unique on a college campus, generally for departmental reasons. If the service is fairly specialized, meeting the needs of a small group of dedicated constituents, it should be evaluated to determine whether it should reside in a department, not in the central IT organization.

It is prudent to evaluate services that have not been changed for a number of years. For example, has the suite of supported software remained static for years? Have the public computing facilities continued as is year after year? An objective evaluation may determine that the services are necessary and well received or may conclude that the services are stagnant and the resources devoted to them would be more strategically deployed in other areas.

Leading change is a challenge! When faced with having to reduce or eliminate well-used services because of resource constraints, it is tempting to try to spread resources just a little thinner or to be all things to all people. The resulting service model resembles a few fingers trying to fill a lot of holes in the levee. A better solution is to consider what can be credibly supported, meeting most needs well rather than meeting all needs poorly. If the service dilutes programmatic focus for the primary organizational mission, it should be considered for elimination. Trimming services to the most necessary and assuring alignment with the most important requirements of the university will provide the best model for service in the long run.

COLLABORATIONS

Perhaps the most profound change in successful service organizations will be the extent to which they collaborate. Collaboration with clients—faculty, students, departments, schools, and support units like libraries and advising centers—should drive the IT service model. IT units should be more concerned about coordinating with their clients and their academic needs and priorities than on technology itself. "Shadow services," or local technology and service programs may arise because central IT organizations are focused on the technology rather than on the user. Chris Ferguson describes this phenomenon in libraries as a Ptolemaic model, where services are rooted to a physical place and physical objects, books in his example, much like the earth at the center of cosmology (2000). The relationship of the reader to the library is one where the user must come to a physical place and seek the help of experts to make use of the resources. The service model used in many IT organizations is similarly self-centered and rooted to technology rather than to the users. Decisions to limit support to one platform or to a few general software applications are convenient for the support organization but rarely consider how a scholar with unique computing needs accomplishes his or her work. This support model revolves around the IT organization, not the faculty and students. Similarly, users may be required to come to physical locations to receive services or to talk to experts about problems with their computers. Technology services rooted to a physical space are increasingly counterproductive, particularly in this age where information resources can be distributed and collaboration via technology is increasingly commonplace.

Critical to the success of the IT organization is the ongoing dialog with members of the user community to assure that the service model is based on their needs. Understanding of academic needs and priorities cannot be gleaned from afar, but rather must be gained by regular interaction at strategic and operational levels. Discussions at the highest levels of the university about technology and programmatic need must be coupled with regular interaction with faculty and students to understand academic priorities and needs. When these communications happen in conjunction with other campus IT organizations, the resulting cohesiveness of services will shape the new organization.

MULTI-TIERED SERVICE MODELS

A successful service organization is multi-tiered, combining a variety of configurations. Multi-tiered models of support are flexible. At the same time, they offer comfortable levels of interaction to users, allowing the service organization to adjust the levels of support based on situational needs. Some types of technology lend themselves more to one mode of service than another, just as different individuals and groups require different kinds of support models. The right mix of support models achieves results that work for the users and allows the service organization to adapt and adjust content and modes easily. There are four common ways to deliver service; the mix and balance of resources devoted to each can be adjusted to provide customization as circumstances dictate.

Centralized support works well for services that must be standardized for the institution, and assures a base of technology expertise within the institution. Centralized support is typically focused on widely used technology and infrastructure. Security-related services, software licensing, and digital collection management lend themselves to an organizational model where the quality and consistency of service can be assured. Infrastructure systems are also well served by central support groups. The earlier suggestion of providing multi-use infrastructure technology implies a strong base of support to maintain and deliver the services to other units. Similarly, centralized support can be effective to introduce specialized technologies such as multimedia or statistical computing. Faculty and students who may not have the hardware and software to complete a task can avail themselves of the technology and of knowledgeable support staff, and evaluate if individual departments need to consider support of these technologies.

Distributed support services are based in departments and other communities and are typically focused on the individual faculty or student. Support staff are available where the faculty and students need them, and they understand the users' particular needs, the academic discipline of the department, and any related specialized computing needs. IT support staff must provide links to the more centralized areas of support, acting as discipline-specific interpreters of technology. This model is particularly effective in student residences, where support is often needed on evenings and weekends, and where technology is intertwined with course work. Having help available at the right time on topics unique to student use of technology is required for a successful support program. It is increasingly important for this type of distributed support to be available to the faculty using instructional technologies, where support can be given in context to the academic discipline of the individual.

Collaborative support is the service model of the future. If the earlier assumption that programmatic deployment of technology-based initiatives is correct, then a support model that enables departments to succeed in these endeavors is in alignment with the institution's needs. The focus is on allowing the department or program as a whole to achieve their goals by collaborating across organizational boundaries. Several examples illustrate this notion.

- The community centers want to have small computer clusters to serve the members of the community. The local unit maintains the hardware. The central IT group extends their computer disk imaging capabilities to the community centers, allowing them to accomplish their programmatic goal without investing in servers and staff who can manage the high-end technology.
- The Composition Department wants to adopt pedagogy that requires technology-enhanced collaborative writing spaces. The IT unit that runs the campus's computer clusters can lend computers and technical expertise to the department to help them develop prototypes for the spaces, allowing the teachers to refine their ideas before large investments are made in new installations of technology. IT support staff in the Composition Department support the faculty directly and serve as liaisons to the central IT organization.

- The humanities center plans to offer grants to students and faculty for interdisciplinary research and teaching projects. During the proposal phase, central IT staff consult with proposal authors about what technology services might be needed to complete their projects, including the identification of local IT support staff. Once the grants are awarded, the IT staff help the recipients navigate the available service offerings (facilities, technology, workshops, consulting services) to build a "collaborative" support program that feels customized while it makes use of existing resources.

Virtual services capitalize on the existing central and distributed services, but take advantage of the technology already used by faculty and students for classes. Web sites for distributing information, discussion sites, and late night assistance via e-mail and chat are commonly promoted as successful enhancements to learning. The same technologies can successfully be used in a support organization in combination with other models. Offering users, especially trained users, the opportunity to receive support through virtual mechanisms is a commonsense solution for making support available when and where it is most helpful to the user.

The most successful support model combines a variety of mechanisms in a multi-tiered structure. Consider this model for comprehensive support of course management systems. During the day, professional staff are available in person and by computer and phone to answer questions or assist in using the system. In the evening and on the weekends, students staff the help desk and are available via the virtual tools. Staff who are distributed to departments can assist in discipline-specific uses of the system, for example, mathematical notation and multilingual support. Student staff can help other students understand how to open document files, take online surveys, use the discussion board, and other activities common to their use of the system. Staff in the central support group will have deeper expertise in all aspects of the system, so they can offer workshops and provide expert help to their colleagues. The support model works in multiple locations, with different structures for different users, day and night, using a variety of mechanisms.

Most IT organizations have already developed practices that facilitate the institution's plans to deploy technology-based systems and provide just-in-time assistance to faculty, students and staff, and they have considerable experience in constructing and delivering service models. Good impact can be made by building on existing strengths, extending core services to more parts of the campus using a variety of support methods.

INNOVATION AROUND THE EDGES

There is a potential conflict between the ideas of building a core of solidly supported services and continually adjusting the organization to meet changing programmatic demands. Adaptability and stability are not mutually exclusive. The compromise is in balancing the amount and pace of change against core service requirements. The core set of services should be stable, well supported, and cleanly delivered. Adaptation of services happens around the edges of the organization, where the capacity to be nimble is greater, and where there is a greater possibility of the objective evaluation of a new offering. Higher education is particularly well suited to prototyping new services or technologies. Because new services are needed, they are also accepted.

One way to innovate is to structure a project-based customization of services. Projects serve as a way to test a new idea or extend a service model but with tight boundaries on the expectations set. The advantages are several:

- Evaluation of a new technology or methodology against real world problems is possible. If successful, the technology or methodology can be extended, and if not successful, altered or discarded.
- Future capabilities can be explored. Often, one project can help inform the planning and implementation of another. Nascent programmatic ideas can be weighed against the project to help better determine costs and viability based on what is learned from the trial.
- Financial impacts can be more manageable. The cost of a project is less than a full-fledged implementation, and future funding can be justified if the project is successful.

- Staff can build mastery of the technology or process before it becomes a production standard.

A project here at Stanford has helped us demonstrate these concepts. A few years ago, the opportunity arose to create a digital collection from a set of unique documents. We undertook the endeavor with two purposes: to digitize the documents, and to try to develop a set of technical and process structures that could be reused on future projects. The project came with existing boundaries that prevented scope creep, most notably that the documents were off-site and could not be moved to campus for scanning. The collection was quite large, and we had limited access to the project site, so production quality and quantity had to be as high as possible. Because of the rigid project boundaries, we were able to define similarly rigid processes and infrastructure for metadata definitions, workflow, and metadata and document capture, as well as for the post-capture process to make the collection available and searchable. This project has allowed us to explore technology and production workflows in a limited setting, adjusting and learning as we progressed. The mechanisms being developed for processing and delivering the documents are intended as a long-term solution for future digital collection projects. After some refinement, the technology and process have been proven reliable, and the production methodology and technology are now being used in other digital library projects. Perhaps most importantly, we have developed a base of knowledge that is being applied to new endeavors.

While projects are a powerful way to innovate around the edges, they must be undertaken with care, to assure they align with the goals of the organization and university. Optimally, a project helps the organization to explore and develop what will be the next area of sustained core services. In the example of our digital collection project, the work was done in our libraries and formed an extension of the existing materials collection efforts. It has served as the foundation for additional digital collection and development efforts.

A second way to innovate in support models is to coordinate them with new ways of learning. Currently, initiatives in project-based and problem-based learning, collaborative teaching efforts, and new requirements for research skills in the digital age are a few of the areas of change in higher education that raise tantalizing questions for support organizations. Will these changing practices require newly configured physical and virtual spaces or different kinds of technical tools? Might new ways of content development and use need to be supported? Will the artifacts of the class need to be presented in different ways? Exploring support and technical responses to these questions will not only serve the immediate needs of the teaching programs but will allow the support organization to gain experience with the new requirements in anticipation of widespread adoption.

This is an area of innovation particularly well suited to collaboration with instructors and students, teaching assistants, and staff. Those directly involved in creating and actualizing the changed pedagogy must drive the change in the support process. Something as simple as engaging students to configure the furniture in group study spaces or to recommend suites of supported software can help assure that services are well aligned to the needs of the end user. Engaging faculty in evaluating technology trials can assure that the final decisions are both relevant to their programs and supportable by the IT organization.

WHERE TO START?

The only way to assure that an IT support organization stays on track is to evaluate its services continually in light of the needs of the university. Services must be assessed continually to assure that they support the university's needs effectively and efficiently. The following key questions should be asked regularly:

Are the essential programs at the institution supported?

Central to the concept of aligning a support service with the mission of the institution is assuring that the needs of key programs are being met. One way to understand what is important to the institution is to ascertain where funding is being directed. If a program is receiving new funding from the institution, then it must be considered in IT support plans. For example, if undergraduate programs are getting strong financial support, aligning IT services to the university's mission might entail support to the departments responsible for the undergraduate initiatives. Alternatively, the IT organization may be able to assure that undergraduates have adequate consulting, training, and computing facilities through centralized programs.

What does the institution think of the IT support services?

Another way to understand what is important to the university seems almost too obvious to mention but is critically important. Ask. Regularly ask what is important to those who rely on the support given, and to those who are responsible for academic programs. Meeting quarterly or semiannually to exchange summaries of major projects and objectives and to brainstorm on shared problems and goals will help identify areas of potential change. One example of this method of alignment is underway at Stanford now. Many months ago, I met with an associate dean to give an overview of our services and to ask what was happening in her area. She spoke about a discussion among faculty about the science and math core curriculum, and I shared with her the kinds of requests we heard from faculty and students in those disciplines. There was no need for a change in our services then, and she was unsure what the outcome of their conversations would be. However, in subsequent months as the faculty conversations progressed, innovative and meaningful ideas have surfaced for the use of technology in support of this important curriculum. The "checking in" conversation led to collaboration between our organizations that is directly aligned with the needs of the university.

Are the IT staff in the communication loop?

An equally important strategy is to gather information internally. In *The Power of Alignment*, Labovitz and Rosansky note that the staff in an organization are often the most knowledgeable about customer needs and perceptions (1997). Staff can act as effective interpreters of institutional need because they have the advantage of seeing and talking with many people. By interpreting and summarizing trends in how services are used, staff can help inform organizational directives. For example, help desk consulting staff will know about common problems, trends in computer usage, or a particular technology that a lot of faculty and students are asking for. Many IT organizations use software tools to gather this data systematically. The information they provide can help surface areas for service adjustment and will help to build an expectation that the organization will regularly change and an understanding that they can motivate change by advocating the needs of the faculty and students. Staff also need to understand what is expected of them. They must have the opportunity to understand the overall purpose of the organization and how their jobs fit within that framework. They must also understand how they are expected to contribute to the success of the organization, and what skills they need to accomplish their work.

As service models are fine-tuned, it is critical to communicate the changes widely. The goals of the organization should be clearly defined and the message delivered consistently and regularly. This is particularly important when services are streamlined. Although it can be difficult to deliver a message that a particular service is ending, transition can open the door to new opportunities and new collaborations. It is through these opportunities and collaborations that transformation will occur. The charge given to the organization of the future is both challenging and compelling: It must be flexible, more attuned to the needs of the institution, and better blended with the academic enterprises. Its efforts must be stable, scalable, and above all, effective. Success will be measured ultimately by how well the university can achieve its goals.

REFERENCES

Ferguson, Chris. 2000. "'Shaking the Conceptual Foundations,' Too: Integrating Research and Technology Support for the Next Generation of Information Service." *College & Research Libraries* 61, no. 4 (July): 300–311.

Labovitz, George and Victor Rosansky. 1997. *The Power of Alignment*. New York: John Wiley & Sons.

FURTHER READINGS

Champy, James. A. 1996. Preparing for Organizational Change. In *The Organization of the Future*, edited by Francis Hesselbein, Marshall Goldsmith, and Richard Beckhard. New York: The Peter F. Drucker Foundation for Nonprofit Management.

Conner, Daryl R. 1998. *Leading at the Edge of Chaos*. New York: John Wiley & Sons.

Hammer, Michael. (1996). The Soul of the Organization, Preparing for Organizational Change. In *The Organization of the Future*, edited by Francis Hesselbein, Marshall Goldsmith, and Richard Beckhard. New York: The Peter F. Drucker Foundation for Nonprofit Management.

Kotter, John P. 1996. *Leading Change*. Boston: Harvard Business School.

Lundin, Rolf A. and Christophe Midler, eds. 1998. *Projects as Arenas for Renewal and Learning Processes*. Boston: Kluwer Academic Publishers.

Part II

Examining Cultural and Organizational Transformation

Chapter 4

Crossing the Great Divide: Implementing Change by Creating Collaborative Relationships

Anne Scrivener Agee
Executive Director of the Division of Instructional and Technology Support Services and Deputy Chief Information Officer

and

Dee Ann Holisky
Associate Dean for Academic Programs, George Mason University

INTRODUCTION: A HOUSE DIVIDED

IT view of academics

Hang around the IT department of just about any college or university and you will hear sentiments like those below.

> "Faculty have such unrealistic expectations about the IT unit and about technology in general."

> "They don't understand how long it takes to implement new technology. They don't know how many people it takes to maintain a technology infrastructure."

> "They read about some new gadget in an airline magazine and expect us to make it available the next day, without any understanding of whether or how it fits with the technology we already have or whether there are better, cheaper, or easier tools to do the same thing."

> "They basically think of the IT unit as servants who should respond instantly to their every whim. They certainly don't think of us as partners, and it wouldn't occur to most faculty members that someone in IT might be able to make an intelligent suggestion about how to do their work more effectively or efficiently."

> "They are often rude to the IT staff, don't listen when the staff tries to explain something to them, and blame the IT staff for everything from electrical power failures to budget cuts."

Academics' view of IT

Hang around the faculty and deans' offices in almost any college or university and you will hear sentiments like those below.

> "The IT unit is so unresponsive. I have to do everything myself."

> "I have a problem with my modem, but I don't have any idea whom to ask for help."

> "The electronic classrooms are so unreliable that I can't plan my class around using technology."

> "The university technology system is either down or so slow that I can't ask my students to do assignments that rely on it."
>
> "Too much of the limited university budget is allocated to technology."
>
> "The IT unit has control over decisions that affect my teaching and research, like what software will be available in the labs, which applications will be offered in the student center, and how much server space I can have for my files/research project."
>
> "I called the help desk but they were rude and treated me like I was an idiot."
>
> "Can you believe it? They want to change the e-mail system in the middle of the semester? Don't they know anything about our teaching schedule?"

It may not stoop to actual name-calling, and it may not amount to open warfare, but the relationship between the IT unit at the university and the academic units is often adversarial. In contrast, specialists in organizational development have long advocated collaboration as essential to successful, high-performance organizations. Stephen R. Covey, for example, describes building relationships as the key to highly effective organizations.

> When two or more organizations work together, achieving win-win is not as hard as it sounds. By attacking a problem from several angles, a mutually beneficial solution will, more often than not, become apparent to both sides. It will be a solution that is better than either organization could find on its own. (1999: 152)

Similarly, James M. Kouzes and Barry Z. Posner, after studying hundreds of public and private organizations, concluded that

> collaboration has at last assumed its rightful place among the processes for achieving and sustaining high performance. . . . The increasing emphasis on reengineering, world-class quality, knowledge work, and electronic communication, along with the surging number of global alliances and local partnerships, is testimony to the fact that in a more complex, wired world, the winning strategies will be based upon the 'we not I' philosophy. (1995: 152)

With the academic and IT cultures glaring at each other across a great divide, such collaboration within the university may seem like a distant possibility at best. However, collaboration is the key to overcoming the divide and helping both the IT organization and the academic units accomplish the institution's mission more effectively than either could do alone. In order to achieve collaboration, both IT and academic leaders need to commit to, plan for, and model collaborative behavior.

INTERLUDE: SOME CONTEXT ABOUT THE AUTHORS

Before moving on, we would like to give our readers a little context for our discussion of collaboration. We both work at George Mason University in Fairfax, Virginia—Dee as the associate dean for academic programs in the College of Arts and Sciences (CAS) and Anne as the executive director of the Division of Instructional and Technology Support Services (DoIT), part of the Information Technology Unit. George Mason serves 24,000 students, almost 10,000 of them in CAS. Our collaboration began in 1998 when we both started working on the university's Technology Across the Curriculum initiative (TAC). Anne had just started at George Mason then with a directive to develop a new instructional support unit, and Dee had just started her position as associate dean. Since the TAC project is the touchstone of our collaborative work, we mention it often in this chapter. TAC, built around a collaboratively developed set of ten technology goals, is intended to assure that all of our students graduate with fluency in a wide range of technology skills. The project won the 2001 EDUCAUSE award for systemic progress in teaching and learning, and we are convinced that it is the collaborative nature of the project that has led to its continuing success. For more detail about TAC, see our article in the *Educause Quarterly* at www.educause.edu/asp/doclib/abstract.asp?ID=EQM0041 (Agee and Holitsky, 2000).

CULTURAL HISTORY: BARRIERS TO COLLABORATION

So what is it about the cultures of the IT and academic professionals in higher education that has led to such a divide?

First of all, the two cultures have quite different histories in higher education. Academic professionals have hundreds of years of tradition that help to define their roles in the institution. They generally have a strong place in institutional governance and are seen as central to the instructional and research mission of the institution, second only to the students as the core of the university. IT professionals, on the other hand, have a relatively short and somewhat tempestuous history in higher education with role definitions that have changed rapidly in that short time from marginal support to critical institutional function. However, they rarely have a role in institutional governance (and thus seldom interact with faculty in the context of institutional issues) and are not seen as central to the institution's instructional and research mission. This profound difference in roles leads to such interesting phenomena as a standing committee on technology that not only has no representation from the IT unit but rarely even speaks to the IT unit except to issue ultimata about what the university should or should not do with technology.

Because of these different histories, the cultures have different places within the organization of the institution. Their internal structures are not the same, and their heads often report to different senior officers of the institution. Academic units are generally composed of discipline-based departments or programs (for example, the English Department), which are grouped into colleges and schools (for example, the College of Arts and Sciences), whose heads (deans) report to a senior academic officer, often a provost. Given its recent history in academia, it isn't possible to make any generalizations about the internal organization of the IT unit, if, indeed, there is a single central unit. In established institutions, academic departments tend to be relatively stable, but because of the rapid changes in technology, the IT unit frequently changes its structure to reflect changing priorities. (In our own institution, the IT unit has been through two major reorganizations since 1997 following the creation of a new Vice President for Information Technology position.) The head of the IT unit may be at the level of a provost or may be several levels down, with less access to senior-executive-level planning and decision making.

In short, the two cultures live in different organizational worlds, which contributes to the fact that the two sides often do not understand how to interact effectively with each other.

Similarly, professionals in each culture acquire and demonstrate expertise differently and thus members of one group may tend to place lesser value on the expertise of members of the other group. The academic community puts great weight on research and scholarly achievement as measures of expertise, while the IT community puts more weight on practical application and problem-solving abilities. There are few Ph.D.'s in the IT unit, in fact, few graduate degrees of any kind except possibly among the librarians, and technical certifications that are highly regarded by IT professionals carry little weight with academics. A new publication by a faculty member rates a note in the accolades column of the university newspaper, but successful implementation of a new e-mail system is rarely noted as an achievement by the university community. The route to expertise in the academic community is fairly well-defined, while status in the IT community may come through a number of different paths. Each group feels a certain discomfort in the presence of the alien expertise of the other, is unsure how to value it, and as a result, discounts it, or at least values it less than the kind of expertise with which they are more familiar. (This phenomenon may be seen in miniature in the faculty member who does not know how to evaluate a student's multimedia project and either discourages students from doing such projects or rates them lower than traditional research projects where they have a clearer sense of the criteria and feel more expert.)

Related to these different kinds of expertise is the relative emphasis given to individuality and interdependence by the two cultures. Academic scholarship and even teaching are viewed primarily as individual achievements. To be successful, scholars develop original materials and guard their individual interest in their intellectual property. Courses are thought of as "mine." Scholars academic research and teaching is usually not impacted significantly by the work of their colleagues at the institution. Indeed, most faculty are not aware of what their colleagues are researching and still less aware of what their colleagues are doing in the classroom. IT professionals, on the other hand, tend to work more in systems and succeed by understanding how their products and achievements fit into the larger systems of technology at the institution and serve the larger strategic goals of the institution. They have few opportunities to develop individual projects or research an issue simply for the joy of creating new knowledge.

The differing emphases on individuality often lead to different ways of defining problems. Faculty often see technology issues as closed systems. The faculty member finds a software application that will perform a function that he or she needs. The only consideration is whether or not it will perform the needed function and thus solve the faculty member's problem. The IT professional, on the other hand, more likely sees this as an open system. How will the software run on the network? Does it pose a security risk? Does it require specialized support? Is the server capacity sufficient to handle a new application? The IT staff often feels enormous pressure to make change quickly because they are barraged with requests. In such a situation, they are strongly tempted to make decisions in isolation because it is faster and because, after all, they reason, they are far more expert in the technology than the faculty making the requests.

The differences between the two cultures are further compounded by different languages. IT professionals, in particular, are often guilty of using their professional jargon as a tool to keep others away from their domain of expertise, consciously or unconsciously. How many faculty have become convinced that they could never create a Web page because some technology guru has tried to explain the process in intimidating technical detail or insisted on reviewing the minutiae of HTML coding before actually showing someone how to develop a page?

Finally, cultural differences are exacerbated by the huge resource demands of technology. Unless the institution's budget is constantly expanding—a situation that few colleges and universities can claim—the money to support technology is money that used to go to academic programs. And many academics are fiercely resentful of the money being poured into the "black hole" of technology even if they are not hostile to the technology itself. The struggle for scarce resources may prevent collaboration as each group tries to protect its own people and programs from budget cuts.

Given these differences, it is little wonder that the two groups generally carry out their work in separate silos of the institution with collaborative activities few and far between.

The following scenario illustrates this *modus operandi*:
A large academic department, one that happens to be relatively receptive to using technology as a tool to improve productivity, decides to develop a Web-based database application to track students' lab work. Frustrated with attempts to get the IT unit to do this for them, the department hires someone outside the university to develop the application. They arrange for it to be housed on a server maintained by the IT unit and hire a graduate student to track the records generated by the software. He is not trained in the application or made responsible for its maintenance. After several semesters of successful operation, the IT unit does a routine upgrade of the server software, and the database application crashes.

The communication following the software failure exacerbates the situation. Not understanding the internal organization of the IT unit, the initial complaint is made by blanket e-mail to everyone from the head of the IT organization to the graduate assistant who is monitoring the data. The department blames the IT unit for the failure and approaches the dean's office for funds to purchase its own server. The IT unit blames the department for not upgrading its software. A seemingly small technology glitch has even greater repercussions, when, at the end of the semester, the department finds itself without the records necessary to calculate student grades.

In this scenario, except for the moment the locally developed application was loaded on a university-maintained server, each side operated independently of the other. Given the gulf between academics and IT discussed above, this outcome was not surprising, but minimal collaboration before or after might have led to a more successful one. The department could have sought the expertise of the IT staff to understanding better how it could ensure smooth operation of the application over time. The department could have had the student work more closely with the IT unit to become aware of issues involved with software maintenance. The IT unit could have developed guidelines for running applications on their servers. The IT unit could have informed users of the impending upgrade of server software and the potential consequences for people running older applications on the server. Had the department understood the structure of the IT organization better, they might have understood the scope of the problem sooner and been able to fix it before the end of the semester. Had the IT unit understood how this application impacted students, they might have been more diligent in helping the department keep it working.

COLLABORATION: THE KEY TO BRIDGING THE DIVIDE

Leaders in both IT and academic areas can hardly avoid being aware of these cultural differences and the problems they cause, since they are generally confronted by some stunning example on an almost daily basis. The real question for leadership is how to respond to this awareness. Should we simply accept the great divide as a fact of life, hone our conflict-resolution skills, and get on with our work? On the contrary, we suggest that by actively using collaboration as a leadership strategy, both the IT organization and the academic organization can minimize problems like that posed in our scenario and become more successful. Moreover, successful collaboration opens up new possibilities for achievement that are not available to units working alone.

These positive outcomes are possible because, when all is said and done, collaboration itself is the most effective way to overcome the cultural divide. It is our experience that collaborative activities improve mutual understanding, increase respect for the expertise embodied in each organization, open up the possibility of commonly-agreed-upon solutions, enable more effective use of resources, and, as a result of all these, build trust relationships that foster further collaboration.

Although, as noted above, the IT unit and the academic units have very different cultures, working together on projects can improve mutual understanding of the values and structures of each. Our initial collaboration provides a good example. Given funds and tasked with developing an initiative to improve the technology workforce, the IT unit approached the College of Arts and Sciences (CAS) for names of ten faculty members to participate. Their plan was to provide the faculty with training, graduate student assistants, and laptops as an incentive to incorporate technology into their courses. The college did not comply with names but engaged the IT unit instead in a more protracted discussion of the goals of the initiative and alternative ways to achieve those goals.

The CAS leadership cautioned the IT unit that issues like "workforce development," though valued by IT people and the community at large, would not be motivating to the faculty. They suggested framing the project so that it would resonate with faculty, not repulse them. The college also insisted that if wide-scale changes were desired, it was crucial to work with departments and not individual faculty. The IT unit came to realize that the college knew how to work with its faculty more effectively and eventually left much of the management of the program to college administration. This delegation was possible because, through these discussions, it became apparent that the college had also learned. It had developed an appreciation of the different values and needs of the IT unit and the constraints under which it operated and was now willing to work with its staff on the common project. This initial collaboration has fostered many others through which the two units have continued to learn from each other. It was, if you will, our first bridge across the great divide from which we learned the most important lesson that collaboration is our key to mutual success.

Collaborative activities also help bridge the divide between academics and IT because they lead to increased respect for the expertise embodied in each organization. In the previous example, one outcome of the collaboration was that the IT unit came to recognize that the academic side had information that they did not have but that was crucial to the success of their initiative. That is, the academic professionals were the experts in motivating faculty and in the internal organization of the college. The IT unit has since taken advantage of this expertise in numerous other projects.

At the same time, CAS came to appreciate the expertise of the IT unit and has drawn on it at other times. In a recent project, the college turned to the IT unit for help with server security, and this initial consultation resulted in a more extensive look at servers run within the college. Through this collaborative activity, college administrators have developed a much better understanding of the issues involved in running servers, and the IT unit is helping it develop a set of guidelines for server administrators to follow.

A third benefit of collaboration is that it opens up the possibility of commonly-agreed-upon solutions. In a non-collaborative environment, one side makes a unilateral decision that it may or may not even inform the other about. In a collaborative environment, the two sides come together to discuss potential solutions, explore pros and cons of each, and come to a compromise. Not only does this usually result in a better solution, because it has been forged with more information from multiple perspectives, but it often results in smoother implementation because both sides have bought into the solution.

The process of choosing an e-mail system provides an example of the benefits of collaboration. Rather than decide on a system in isolation from the faculty, the IT unit engaged them in a process of collaborative decision making. From the first phase of deciding who should participate in the process, through setting the parameters for the system and weighing the pros and cons of available systems, to a jointly run pilot project and a final decision, the IT unit and the academic units were equal partners. That partnership set the stage for cooperation on the implementation of the new system as well, which proceeded more smoothly than one would expect, in large part due to the fact that key faculty in departments had been involved all along and felt ownership in the project.

Collaboration between the IT unit and academic units can also lead to more efficient use of limited resources. This involves obvious things like pooling resources for software purchases to enable volume discounts or site license purchases that neither unit could manage on its own. It can also involve less obvious activities such as our recent collaboration on the outfitting of an electronic classroom. The faculty could not easily implement a curricular change because it required a specialized classroom. The funds for equipment purchase were provided by CAS since it had a small surplus, but the cost of installation and maintenance was picked up by the IT unit. In another case, CAS needed to provide support to faculty who wanted to incorporate database assignments into their courses. The IT unit provided the staff, but the college paid for the additional training they would need to be able to assist the faculty adequately.

A final benefit to collaboration between IT and academics is that successful activities led to the development of trust between the two units. In our experience, a strong, mutual trust has led naturally to further collaboration. Every collaboration described above led to further collaboration at a deeper, more significant level. Moreover, collaborative activities will lead to a culture of collaboration, opening up possibilities that couldn't have been envisioned earlier. For example, the university has recently been asked by the state to develop standards for student performance in IT skills. The four committees working on setting these standards include both faculty and members of the IT staff, a situation that would have been unimaginable even two or three years ago. But, because of the history of collaborative activities, the faculty acknowledged that the IT staff, who in fact provide hands-on technology training for thousands of students, had something important to offer to the discussion.

Probably all institutions suffer from some version of the great divide between the academic units and the IT unit; at least it is true in the institutions with which we are familiar. Because of this divide, neither side is as successful as it has the potential to be, and precious resources are often wasted. It is therefore reasonable to expect that all institutions would take an active interest in bridging the divide. Although it seems at first glance that the existence of the divide provides a reason for not collaborating, we argue that collaboration itself is the most effective way to cross it.

FIRST REQUISITE FOR COLLABORATION: PLANNING

As we have indicated, we think collaboration is a good idea, but that belief by itself is not enough to make it work. Good collaboration needs to be actively planned for, especially in the beginning, if it is to be effective in changing the paradigm we have described above.

First, we believe that collaboration needs to start at the top. The leaders in the IT and academic organizations need to encourage, facilitate, and model collaborative behavior if they want to reap the maximum benefits of the strategy. It is certainly possible that collaboration could be initiated at other levels in the organization, but without the support and encouragement of the leadership, it will be difficult and probably not as effective as it could otherwise be.

In our own case, we can point to our Technology Across the Curriculum initiative as an excellent example of this principle. When this program started, both the IT unit and the College of Arts and Sciences (CAS) were involved, but each area performed its part without a great deal of interaction with the other. CAS would let the IT unit know what it needed, and the IT unit would provide the requested service. Although the program had the strong backing of the leadership in both units, the contacts for the respective programs were several levels removed from the top leadership. About a year into the program, the dean of CAS and the vice president for information technology suggested that the head of academic programs and the executive director of instructional technology should take a more active role in leading the initiative together, including meeting regularly to make decisions about the direction of the program. At that point, the program began to be a truly collaborative one, and its success improved dramatically as a result. The IT unit gained a better understanding of the goals of the program and had a hand in shaping those goals and the strategies used to meet them. CAS realized that there were many additional resources available that had not so far been tapped to support the program. The leaders in both units made it clear throughout their respective organizations that the TAC initiative was important to both areas and that projects related to TAC were to be given high priority.

In the example above, the leaders took advantage of an existing program to encourage collaboration, but leaders may also need to create opportunities for collaboration beyond those that may present themselves in the ordinary course of work.

The organizational leaders are in the best position to initiate the structures that will support collaborative efforts and change the procedures or policies that may inhibit collaboration. This kind of action may be something as simple as making sure that information about whom to contact for what kind of project is readily available to all parties through Web sites, brochures, bulletin boards, or other means. Or it may be as complex as reorganizing the IT unit to put more emphasis on communication and customer service. It may even involve the development of an entirely new structure. In George Mason's case, one of the outgrowths of the collaborative efforts of the Technology Across the Curriculum initiative was the creation of an informal assessment council that brought together IT staff, institutional assessment staff, and CAS faculty and administrators, all of whom had an interest in measuring the achievements of the TAC program. That group has planned a new assessment Web page, helped develop faculty training in assessment techniques, and served as a sounding board for various assessment strategies related to the TAC initiative. The assessment council represents an entirely new structure for bringing together several kinds of interest and expertise about assessment that would not otherwise have coalesced to serve the institution.

In addition, organizational leaders are in the best position to create a collaborative mind-set in the organization, consciously and deliberately putting a value on collaboration. Leaders create this mind-set by encouraging departments within their units to set collaborative goals, by including collaboration as part of the charge to committees and task forces, by defining collaboration as part of staff job descriptions and performance evaluations, and by insisting on feedback mechanisms as part of any solution. If there is a collaborative mind-set, then no report is accepted unless it has clear buy-in from all the affected parties. Note that this collaborative mind-set goes somewhat against the grain of the "expert" mentality mentioned earlier. Both academics and IT professionals may be more in the habit of telling people what should be done—in their expert opinion—than of soliciting input and truly understanding what the other group needs to solve a particular problem or do its job more effectively. In truth, it often takes more than one kind of expertise to understand and solve a problem, academic or technological.

Leaders are also in a position to choose activities for collaboration—set the pace, as it were. It may not be possible or desirable to do everything collaboratively, especially in a culture where it is not especially encouraged. But some activities should be consciously chosen by the organization because of their collaborative value. In picking activities, especially at first, it is helpful to focus on a product or an event and avoid areas of activity that involve turf, resources, etc. For example, George Mason's IT unit regularly hosts campus dialog sessions. Some of these focus specifically on IT issues and are led by IT staff or administrators, but others have involved invited guests from the provost's office or CAS or even the facilities department to lead a discussion about issues where IT has collaborated on a project like a new academic building. In another example, the IT unit partnered with the provost's office, student services, CAS, and student government to sponsor an annual celebration of student learning featuring interactive displays of student work (which might or might not be technology related).

Beyond these basic kinds of collaborative events, of course, lies more complex and sophisticated programmatic collaboration involving more commitment and more resources from the partners. For example, in a recent budget year, four different departments from three schools in the university requested funds to develop four multimedia production facilities. Instead of turning down all four requests for lack of funds, the vice president for information technology volunteered the IT unit to coordinate the collaborative development of a single facility that would meet the needs of all the departments. The group—which included representatives from the IT unit, CAS, the Graduate School of Education, and the School of Fine and Performing Arts—spent a year planning an acceptable facility and defining staffing needs. In the course of the planning year, the team found a lot of previously unknown common ground in the kinds of projects each department or school wanted to carry out in the facility. With this common ground, they were able to provide sophisticated multimedia equipment they all could take advantage of as well as a continuing collaborative structure that would help set scheduling and resource priorities for the facility and work with the new director (also hired collaboratively) to establish policy and procedures. The new media lab is managed by the IT unit with the participation of the cross-unit steering committee, a structure not found anywhere else in the university.

Finally, leaders have to model in their own actions the collaborative mind-set they hope to create within their organization. The leaders have to make time in their calendars for collaborative meetings and spend the time necessary to really understand the organization and the goals of the units with which they expect to collaborate. The leaders have to make public statements about their collaborative efforts. The leaders have to set goals for the organization that include collaboration.

SECOND REQUISITE FOR COLLABORATION: COMMUNICATION

Collaborative relationships, like all good relationships, depend on clear, open, and regular communication. Open channels of communication provide the basic groundwork for enabling collaboration in the first place, while regularized communication with feedback loops is crucial for the success of specific collaborative activities. Strategically planned communication provides the mechanism for supporting successful collaboration in the long run.

To foster a climate of collaboration, each side should ensure that its structures and processes are as transparent as possible and that it has communicated them to the community at large. As a support unit, the IT area is particularly obligated to make sure that its policies, procedures, and services are clearly articulated and easily available to the community they serve. George Mason, for example, has had for a number of years an excellent instructional video production team at GMU-TV whose products consistently bring in national awards for their high quality. But for every finished product, there were many unfinished ones. The television crew would reserve production time only to find that faculty hadn't finished the scripts or didn't show up for taping. The faculty were then very annoyed when the project couldn't be completed because subsequent production time had already been booked for another project.

Finally, GMU-TV realized that it was at least partly to blame for the frustrations since there was really no place that the process was explained to the faculty. Small wonder that faculty did not understand what was expected of them. Three years ago, GMU-TV published a set of guidelines for requesting video production services. The guidelines laid out the process so that faculty would understand how long a production would take and what they needed to contribute to the process. Thus the academic departments could really take advantage of the expertise of the video team to help them showcase their expertise in their own disciplines. Now, every video project begins with a consultation that helps to clarify expectations on both sides and establishes a realistic time frame for the production that allows both the video team and the faculty to use their respective expertise to best advantage.

Beyond the general principle that information needs to be available in order to allow collaboration, the communication needs to be targeted to the right person or people if collaboration is to take place at the appropriate level. If communication has not taken place between the right set of people, then collaboration is as far away as ever. In the scenario detailed above about departmental development of a database application, a staff person in the IT unit may have told the independent software developer about the need for software upgrades, but since the contractor was a temporary player who was communicating with a graduate student, a position which rotated annually, the information was lost. No faculty member or permanent staff person was fully aware of the technical needs and also part of the regular communication with the IT unit. Alternatively, in the case of the TAC program, the real cooperation between the IT unit and the college began only when the heads of the two units began to communicate with each other. Discussions between staff at other levels had generally led to misunderstanding and frustration, resulting mainly in failure of both communication and collaboration.

In addition, communication needs to be regular and regularized. Even when an IT unit and academic unit recognize the need to communicate on a specific issue or project, they may not realize what it takes to communicate successfully over the life of a project. It is important to build communication and feedback into the time line for development and implementation and to determine at the start who is going to be responsible to see that it happens. In investigating the serious problems caused by the software failure in the scenario discussed above, the administration learned that at the beginning of the project, there had been a meeting between the IT server unit and the academic department. The parameters for the collaboration were laid out, and it was agreed to keep in contact as the software was developed and implemented. In spite of these good intentions, that was the only communication between the two until the software crash several semesters later. This might have been avoided had the mechanism for communication and parties responsible for it been worked out at that initial meeting.

Like collaboration, communication does not just happen, and it isn't sufficient simply to value it. Communication takes both planning and follow-through. For any specific activity, a good leader needs to ask, "Who needs to be informed and when? Who needs to give input or feedback and when? Who should be part of the planning? Who needs to be brought in to help implement?" And, most important, "Who is going to be responsible for communication?" Without someone specifically accountable for maintaining the communication—calling the meetings, writing up agendas and summaries, sending out announcements, and reporting back to the unit leader—it is all too easy for each side to fall back into its isolated mode of operation.

The leaders should also look at their units as a whole to determine which people or groups should be communicating on an ongoing basis to ensure smooth operations. They also need to decide explicitly the forms that communication should take—from passive mechanisms like posting information on a Web site or sending a blanket all-staff or all-faculty e-mail or newsletter, to more proactive efforts like scheduled e-chats or standing meetings. A key factor in our successful collaboration has been our development of various regularized modes of communication. Our IT unit and the TAC program both have developed rich Web sites that are updated frequently. The instructional division of the IT unit distributes a regular (paper and online) newsletter to faculty, while the TAC administrators maintain a listserv for updating TAC faculty, students, and staff. The TAC program has meetings once a semester for the TAC faculty and students and includes the IT staff. Finally, the two of us, as heads of the programs, have biweekly meetings to ensure that our units keep in close touch on their program developments.

Regardless of the specific methods, it is important to plan for communication by thinking explicitly about who needs to be part of the communication network, how frequent it needs to be, and what activities would be most effective. In sum, strategically planned communication provides the mechanism for supporting successful collaboration in the long run.

CONCLUSION: BENEFITS OF WORKING TOGETHER

We began this article with a series of comments one might overhear in a typical university setting, one where the IT unit and academic faculty work largely in isolation from one another. In sharp contrast, in a setting where collaboration is valued, planned, and communicated, we have heard the following:

> "They helped us test the software we wanted, and we found a really good application."

> "They helped me locate software for annotating texts and will even load it on their servers and help us troubleshoot it. This will be great for our literature classes."

> "The workshop on WebCT sponsored by the IT unit gave me a lot of new ideas for my classes."
>
> "They arranged for us to meet with the department so we could explain the new system to all the faculty at the same time."
>
> "They gave us good suggestions for changing the classroom configuration so that it would be easier for them to teach."
>
> "The new guidelines the IT unit developed for servers were really helpful. They prevented us from making some serious mistakes on our own."

Where would most people rather work?

By choosing collaboration as a strategy, leaders in the new age of higher education can minimize conflict between two major players in their institutions, leverage limited financial and personnel resources to accomplish more, and bring to bear a powerful tool for organizational and institutional change.

REFERENCES

Agee, Anne Scrivener and Dee Ann Holisky. 2000. Technology Across the Curriculum at George Mason University. *Educause Quarterly*, 23, no. 4: 6–12. [Online]. Available: *www.educause.edu/asp/doclib/abstract.asp?ID=EQM0041*.

Covey, Stephen R. 1999. The Mind-Set and Skill-Set of a Leader. Pp. 149–158 in *Leading Beyond the Walls: How High Performing Organizations Collaborate for Shared Success*, edited by Frances Hesselbein, Marshall Goldsmith, and Iain Somerville. San Francisco: Jossey-Bass.

Kouzes, James M. and Barry Z. Posner. 1995. *The Leadership Challenge: How to Keep Getting Extraordinary Things Done in Organizations*. San Francisco: Jossey-Bass.

Chapter 5

Exploring Cultural Challenges to the Integration of Technology

Jo Ann Carr
Director of the Center for Instructional Materials and Computing, School of Education, University of Wisconsin-Madison

Once upon a time there was a university where the arts and sciences faculty had pledged their loyalty to the content disciplines. To fulfill this troth they scoured relentlessly through the undergraduate rabble in an unrelenting quest to identify a few trustworthy squires who would carry forth the banner of academic specialization and research. Meanwhile, in another sector of the university, lived the education faculty. The education faculty who, having sworn their loyalty to the values of K to 12 education, now also felt allegiance to higher education and thus clamored to have their brethren in arts and sciences honor the discipline of pedagogy. Into this university rode a new provost who decreed "Thou shalt swear thy allegiance to the integration of technology in thy teaching." And they all lived, less than happily, ever after.

This fairy tale, like all myths, contains elements of the truths that must be considered if higher education is to meet the imperative for technology integration. These truths include cultural conflict within the university. This essay will explore the cultural conflict between arts and sciences and teacher education in light of the impact that the integration of technology in teaching and learning will have on higher education. The collaborative integration of technology throughout the content and pedagogy courses in higher education is important because of the sheer impact of teacher education on the American economy and the pervasiveness of teacher education in institutions of higher education. Teacher education programs exist in more four-year institutions than any other professional preparation programs. For example, there are 1287 teacher education programs as contrasted with 243 engineering programs (Clifford, 1988: 38–39). To date, teachers have represented the largest group of knowledge workers in society. In our knowledge economy, the learning needs of teachers are mirrored by many other professions and disciplines.

THE TECHNOLOGY IMPERATIVE

> The best information technology closely parallels the pedagogical goals of the learning paradigm: 1) fostering active learning, 2) constructing knowledge and 3) assessment. (Buckley, 2002: 30)

American higher education has its roots in many cultures—the academies of the seventeenth and eighteenth centuries, the normal schools of the nineteenth and early twentieth centuries, the land grant universities of the 1850s, and the traditions of the European research university. These multiple histories have had varying impacts on the component institutions of American higher education, namely, liberal arts colleges, comprehensive colleges and universities, and research universities, as well as on their school, college, and departmental structures. The imperative for the integration of technology in teaching also stems from multiple sources including the pervasiveness of technology in other areas of society, the demands for accountability from government and business, and attempts by the for-profit virtual universities to assume responsibility for the credentialing that has long been the province of traditional non-profit higher education. The convergence of these forces has prompted Peter Drucker to predict that universities will die in thirty years (Bork, 2000: 81).

The validity of Drucker's prediction is certainly open to question. However, his prediction is based on an assumption that the current structure and mission of higher education does not meet the needs of the contemporary social and economic environment. The integration of technology into higher education can prevent this predicted demise by positioning the university to be more responsive to the needs of society. However, this integration will require faculty transformation and institutional change. Technology can serve as a "lever" in the transformation of higher education as it responds to the needs for active learning, cooperative learning, multiple intelligences, diverse learning styles, interdisciplinary instruction, authentic learning and assessment, critical thinking and problem solving, brain-compatible learning, and our multicultural society (Brown, 2000; Chickering and Ehrmann, 2001; Darling-Hammond, 1999; Diaz, 2000; Sokolow, 1997). The importance of learner needs over technology is echoed by Gandolfo, who states, "The only value of technology for instruction is if it enhances learning in ways that are not otherwise available" (1998: 31).

The movement from a teaching paradigm to a learning paradigm will require a change in the role of the faculty. A focus on teaching requires an understanding of content whereas a focus on learning requires "knowledge of the subject matter, of students and the relationship between the two" (McDiarmid, 1992: 268–269).

The movement to this new focus on learning and the integration of technology will not be easy. The 1999 Campus Computing Survey indicated that 39% of respondents see instructional integration as the biggest challenge. Technology has the potential to move the university to a learner-centered environment; however, our faculty have spent their academic lives and found success in teacher-centered environments. This transformation can only occur when technology is seen as a "catalyst rather than a panacea" (Gandolfo, 1998: 29) and the university truly values collaboration. Teacher education in modern universities is built upon a triumvirate of content, pedagogy, and classroom practice that could provide a model for the collaboration needed to fulfill the transformative power of technology in education.

ROLE OF THE UNIVERSITY IN TEACHER EDUCATION

In *To Touch the Future,* the American Council of Education emphasized the leadership role that college and university presidents must take in making certain that the teachers who are prepared at their institutions are "knowledgeable about *what* they teach and proficient in *how* they teach" (1999: 4). The ACE action agenda cites the need for college presidents to lead arts and sciences and education faculty in combining their contributions of content and pedagogy and in ensuring that teachers are adequately prepared to understand and apply technology to teaching (1999: 7–9). The report goes on to note "the public's perception of entire institutions will be influenced by the perceived quality of teacher education programs and graduates" (1999: 17). W. Ann Reynolds further emphasizes the central role that arts and science faculty play in teacher education by encouraging college and university presidents to place "responsibility for the subject-matter competence of prospective teachers on the shoulders of the academic department faculty" (1997: 114).

The American Council on Education has presented a mandate for leadership from college and university presidents to make decisions about teacher education and the "power to allocate resources to reflect a policy of overall campus responsibility for teacher education" (Jones, 1997: 126). However, fulfilling that mandate and those powers first requires an understanding of the differing cultures of arts and science and teacher education.

TALE OF TWO CULTURES

> Higher education honors the teachers but not the formal pedagogies of teaching.

Many authors have speculated on the reasons for the differences in culture and values of arts and science and those of professional studies. Sally Frost Mason attributes this difference to the conflict between the winnowing process of higher education with its reliance on the bell curve and the "no child left behind" philosophy of K to 12 education (Mason, 2000). The recent and ongoing emphasis in K to 12 education on standards-based education that presupposes a core set of knowledge that all students can and must attain may exacerbate this difference in values.

Charles Avinger and Mary Ann Tighe attribute the conflict to a lack of clear communication, isolation from one another within the university environment, misunderstanding of values and cultures and longstanding prejudices stemming from the historical development of liberal arts and professional programs in American higher education (1994: 172). This difference in history is further explored by Madeline Grumet, who notes the early association of liberal studies with those from the upper class and its resultant identification with privilege and power. In contrast, professionalism, with its origins in apprenticeships, technical training programs, and normal schools has been perceived as a narrow, applied, and highly specialized path to the achievement of higher social status for the students who complete these programs (1995: 7).

Faculty members in the arts and sciences, for the most part, possess a disciplinary identity as a result of their indoctrination in the traditions of academe as they progress through undergraduate, masters, and doctoral studies in the same or closely aligned fields. In contrast, most teacher education faculty have experienced a previous professional life in K to 12 education and thus have a professional as well as disciplinary loyalty. School of Education faculty must answer to both higher education and K to 12 constituencies (Ducharme, 1997). The allegiance of arts and science faculty to the values of academe results in higher education contributing "to the singular scope and purpose of faculty by rewarding most those who most closely follow the traditional rites and rituals" (Ducharme, 1997: 73). This reward system is demonstrated by hiring processes that seek to ensure continuity in the values of the academy and the focus on sabbaticals that ensure that faculty can continue to "do what they are already doing" (Ducharme, 1997: 73).

Roland B. Howsan claims the culture of the disciplines and the culture of the professions are different but highly functional within their own spheres. Faculty in the disciplines value pure forms of research, place value on and reward that pure research, identify with the scholars in their discipline, and value theory over application (1976: 58). Faculty in the professions also value and reward research but are more interested in the application of knowledge, focus on multidisciplinary studies, and relate to both faculty and practitioners (1976: 58–59).

THE IMPACT OF TECHNOLOGY ON FACULTY CULTURES

The imperative to integrate technology into higher education brings a third set of values into this environment. The values of the academy have been defined as academic freedom, self-regulated government, cautious change, a view of the campus as the primary locale for teaching, a standardized learning environment, and faculty advancement based on the building of knowledge rather than the building of learners (Olcott and Schmidt, 2000: 261–263). Contrast the values supported by technology with its rapid change: the use of multiple locales and resources for teaching and learning, a view of content not as knowledge but as a commodity, collaborative learning, customized delivery with a departure from seat time to anywhere/anytime learning, and the support of a learner-centered environment (Matthews, 1998). Olcott has also identified the impact of technology on the traditional norms of higher education as requiring greater flexibility, the integration of research, teaching, and service in determining faculty advancement, and a focus on outcomes and productivity to define success (2000: 264). The role of the teacher in a digital environment will require a greater emphasis on content, counseling, and instructional design skills and may require the sharing of faculty to meet demands for distributed expertise and interdisciplinary studies.

The impact of technology varies by academic area and in its application to research, teaching, and service. A review of these applications provides an indication of the power of technology to bring an intersection to these three roles of higher education. Technology is transforming scholarship through the use of the Internet for information sharing, information retrieval, and collegial communication and collaboration (Baldwin, 1998: 10–11). Technology is transforming service and outreach through applications to real world problems, accessibility of resources that is not limited by time or distance, and the breaking down of barriers between the tools of higher education and the tools of the community (Baldwin, 1998: 11–12). Teaching can also be transformed through information sharing and retrieval, through the creation of collaborative learning communities based in real world settings, and through the use of technology to support new educational needs.

Variation in the impact of technology in academic areas results from differences in the availability of discipline-specific information sources, hardware, software, services, and rewards. The adoption of technology is also affected by faculty members' understanding of and commitment to critical thinking and problem solving. In a 1996 study, Richard W. Paul and his colleagues examined the teaching practices and knowledge about critical thinking within arts and science and education faculty. He defines critical thinking as "thinking that explicitly aims at well-founded judgment and hence utilizes appropriate evaluation standards in the attempt to determine the true worth, merit or value of something" (1997: 3). He found that although arts and science faculty "better articulated the basic skills of thought that students need to effectively address issues and concerns in their lives" (1997: 6), education faculty placed a greater emphasis on problem solving, the role of critical thinking in meeting change and making decisions, and the importance for peer- and self-assessment of learning. He also found that, regardless of discipline, most faculty "intuitively grasp critical thinking" (1997: 7) and recommended that institutions provide training to "enable faculty to reconceptualize the design of their instruction so as to bring intellectual quality, intellectual discipline and intellectual standards into the heart of instruction" (1997: 8).

Differences in the current embrace of good practices in undergraduate education were also noted in a study that involved faculty from mathematics, science, and teacher education. Teacher education faculty promoted active and collaborative learning and respected diverse talents and ways of learning. Arts and science faculty stressed the importance of university values and were more significantly involved in encouraging student-faculty contact. As Powers emphasizes, "Before any legitimate improvement in the professional education of teachers can be operationalized, both teacher education and letters and science faculty must identify and recognize their respective contributions to that practice" (1993: 17–18). The intersection between the roles of education and arts and science faculty was articulated by Maher and Tetreault, who observed that pedagogy does not dilute content "so much as contextualize it" (1999: 41).

MODELS

Although some efforts for the improvement of teacher education have represented the efforts of education and arts and science faculty working independently of one another, two national efforts have focused on a collaborative approach. The Project 30 Alliance supports individual campus efforts for collaboration among faculty (Project 30 Alliance, 2001), and the American Association of Universities (AAU) June 1999 Resolution on Teacher Education strives to "more fully integrate teacher education and professional development programs into the rest of the university" (AAU, 1999).

The Project 30 Alliance requires the collaboration of arts and science faculty with faculty in education. The Alliance supports projects at universities throughout the United States. A review of the 17 current projects of the Alliance indicates that projects at Bridgewater State College, Millersville University, and Albany State University include technology integration or competence in their collaboration projects (Project 30 Alliance, 2001).

The intent of the AAU resolution was forwarded during a two-day Invitational Forum on Exemplary Practices and Challenges in Teacher Education on September 30–October 2, 2001. This forum brought together Deans of Science, Deans of Education, and at least one faculty member with a deep interest in improving teacher education. The forum included a discussion of collaborations among faculty to integrate strong content knowledge and effective classroom practice (AAU, 2001).

Efforts at individual institutions have also addressed collaboration between arts and science and education faculty (Anderson et al., 2000; Barce et al., 2000; de Caprariis, et al., 2000;

Clark et al., 1992; Rothenberg, 1995), but only a few recently have also introduced the third element of technology.

The TACCOL (Technology Advancing a Continuous Community of Learners) project at Clarion University of Pennsylvania focused on "infusing technology into teacher preparation by integrating technology with an interdisciplinary approach to teaching science and mathematics" (Carbone, 2000: 3). This infusion was accomplished through faculty seminars based on the ten teaching principles of quantitative literacy and led faculty in the development workshops to replace the traditional lecture.

Tufts University has also addressed the collaborative integration of technology into teacher education through a program funded by the Fund for Improvement of Postsecondary Education (FIPSE). The Tufts project focused on using "guided inquiry, peer collaboration and modern technology" in changing the way science is taught in schools. Equipment, software, and information resources were used for data collection and analysis that provided virtual active learning experiences not possible in the physical environment (FIPSE, 2002).

The Renaissance Group, a national consortium of 16 colleges and universities, engaged in a five-year project to reform teacher education. Among the principles of the group is "The university prepares teachers to appropriately use technology and interactive strategies to promote student learning" (O'Neal et al., 2000: 3). One of the unanticipated challenges of the group was the amount of time, effort, and resources needed to recruit arts and science faculty to the program, despite the strong administrative support given to teacher education at each campus.

LESSONS LEARNED AND NEXT STEPS

The integration of technology into a collaborative view of teacher education must surmount the differences in culture and values held by arts and science faculty and education faculty. The need for faculty development in reconceptualizing the role of the faculty member and in deepening an understanding of instructional design must also be addressed. The collaborative integration of technology requires champions to model and support it. The continued efforts of the Project 30 Alliance and the renewed commitment of the American Association of Universities can advance this agenda on the national level. However, individual institutions must also commit themselves to a systemic approach and embrace the seven principles for good practice in undergraduate education. Such practice

1. encourages contact between students and faculty,
2. develops reciprocity and cooperation among students,
3. encourages active learning,
4. gives prompt feedback,
5. emphasizes time on task,
6. communicates high expectation, and
7. respects diverse talents and ways of learning (Chickering and Ehrmann, 2000: 1).

The value of technology is its ability to leverage these practices of contact between students and faculty, reciprocity and cooperation among students, active learning techniques, prompt feedback, time on task, communication of high expectations, and respect for diverse talents and ways of learning (Chickering and Ehrmann, 2000). In an age when large segments of the population are joining teachers as knowledge workers, all faculty must serve as models for excellence in teaching and learning.

REFERENCES

American Council on Education. 1999. *To Touch the Future: Transforming the Way Teachers Are Taught: An Action Agenda for College and University Presidents*. Washington, D.C.: American Council on Education.

Association of American Universities. 1999. *AAU Resolution on Teacher Education*. [Online]. Available: *www.aau.edu/education/TeacherEdRes.html*. [8 March 2002].

Association of American Universities (AAU). 2002. *Status of Current Projects: AAU Undergraduate Education Committee*. [Online]. Available: *www.aau.edu/education/Summary4.01.html* [8 March 2002].

Anderson, Marla, David Cole, Fritz Fischer, and Chris Ingram. 2000.

"The Shared Vision and Practice of a University/School Partnership." Paper presented at the 52nd annual meeting of the American Association of Colleges for Teacher Education, Chicago, Ill., February 26–29. ERIC Document Reproduction Service, ED 440 074.

Avinger, Charles, and Mary Ann Tighe. 1994. "Partnerships That Work: Toward Effective Collaboration for In-service Education." *Educational Horizons* (Summer): 170–175.

Baldwin, Roger. G. 1998. Technology's Impact on Faculty Life and Work. Pp. 7–21 in *The Impact of Faculty Life and Work*. New Directions in Teaching and Learning, no. 76. San Francisco: Jossey-Bass.

Barce, Jennifer, et al. 2000. "The One, Two Punch: General Education and Teacher Education Curricula at a Small, Independent Liberal Arts College for All Students Including Pre-service Teachers." Paper presented at the 52nd annual meeting of the American Association of Colleges for Teacher Education, Chicago, Ill., February 26–29. ERIC Document Reproduction Service, ED 440661.

Bork, Alfred. 2000. "Learning Technology." *Educause Review* 35, no. 1. (January/February): 74–85.

Brown, Justine K. 2000. "States of Progress: Education Leaders Talk Technology." *Converge* 3, no. 4 (April): 54–58.

Buckley, Donald P. 2002. "In Pursuit of the Learning Paradigm: Coupling Faculty Transformation and Institutional Change." *Educause Review* 37, no. 1 (January-February): 28-38.

Carbone, Rose E. 2000. "Collaboration between the College of Arts and Sciences and the College of Education at Clarion University of Pennsylvania." Paper presented at the 52nd annual meeting of the American Association of Colleges for Teacher Education, Chicago, Ill., February 26–29. ERIC Document Reproduction Service, ED 440070.

Chickering, Arthur W. and Stephen C. Ehrmann. 2001. "Implementing the Seven Principles: Technology as Lever." [Online]. Washington, D.C.: American Association for Higher Education. Available: *www.aahe.org/technology/ehrmann.htm* [8 March 2002].

Clark, Linda, et al. 1992. "Project 30 and the Pedagogy Seminars: A Report to the Administration and Faculty." ERIC Document Reproduction Service, ED 368687.

Clifford, Geraldine Jonich and James W. Guthrie. 1988. *Ed School: A Brief for Professional Education*. Chicago: University of Chicago Press.

Darling-Hammond, Linda. 1999. "Educating Teachers: The Academy's

Greatest Failure or Its Most Important Future." *Academe* 85, no. 1 (February): 26–33.

de Capraiis, Pascal, Charles Barman, and Paula Magee. 2000. *A Collaborative Effort Between Education and Science Faculty to Improve the Education of Prospective Public Services Teachers.* Annual Meeting of the Association for Educators in Teaching Science, Cleveland, Ohio.

Diaz, David P. 2000. "Technology Training for Educators: The Pedagogical Priority." *CUE Newsletter* 22, no. 2, 1: 25-27.

Ducharme, Edward R. 1997. Developing Existing Education Faculty. In *Strengthening Teacher Education: The Challenges to College and University Leaders,* edited by Peter C. Magrath and Robert L. Egbert, et al. San Francisco: Jossey-Bass (Jossey-Bass Higher Education Series), 71-86.

FIPSE Programs. 1998. Grant P116B970542: Tufts University: Student Oriented Science: Enabling Teachers to Meet the National Science Education Standards. FIPSE Web Site. [Online]. Available: *www.ed.gov/offices/OPE/FIPSE/98ProgBK/Tufts/Thornton.html.* [8 March 2002].

Gandolfo, Anita. 1998. Brave New World? The Challenges of Technology to Time-honored Pedagogies and Traditional Structures. In *Impact of Technology on Faculty Development, Life and Work,* edited by Kay Herr Gillespie. New Directions in Teaching and Learning, no. 76. San Francisco: Jossey-Bass.

Grumet, Madeline. 1995. "Lofty Actions and Practical Thoughts: Education with a Purpose." *Liberal Education* 81, no. 1: 4–11.

Howsan, Robert B., ed. 1976. *Education a Profession: Report of the Bicentennial Commission on Education for the Profession of Teaching of the American Association of Colleges for Teacher Education.* Washington, D.C.: AACTE.

Jones, Linda Bunnell. 1997. Building Campus-wise Support for Teacher Education. In *Strengthening Teacher Education: The Challenges to College and University Leaders,* edited by Peter C. Magrath and Robert L. Egbert, et al. San Francisco: Jossey-Bass. (Jossey-Bass Higher Education Series).

Maher, Frances and Mary Kay Tetreault. 1999. "Knowledge versus Pedagogy: The Marginalization of Teacher Education." *Academe* 85, no. 1 (February): 40–43.

Mason, Sally Frost. 2000. Do Colleges of Liberal Arts and Sciences Need Schools of Education? In *Politics of Teacher Education Reform: The National Commission on Teaching and America's Future.* One Thousand Oaks, Calif.: Corwin.

Matthews, Dewayne. 1998. "Transforming Higher Education: Implications for State Higher Education Finance Policy." *Educom Review* 33, no. 5 (September–October): 48–57.

McDiarmid, G. Williamson. 1992. "The Arts and Sciences as Preparation for Teaching." East Lansing, Mich.: National Center for Teaching and Learning. ERIC Document Reproduction Service, ED 348 358.

Olcott, Donald and Kathy Schmidt. 2000. Redefining Faculty Policies and Practices for the Digital Age. In *Higher Education in an Era of Digital Competition*, edited by Donald E. Hanna. Madison, Wis.: Atwood Press.

O'Neal, Marcia, et al. 2000. "Evaluation of the Renaissance Project for Improving Teacher Quality." Paper presented at the annual meeting of the Mid-South Educational Research Association, Bowling Green, Ken., November 15–17. ERIC Document Reproduction Service, ED 448131.

Paul, Richard W., et al. 1997. "Teachers of Teachers: Examining Preparation for Critical Thinking." Paper presented at the annual meeting of the American Education Research Association, Chicago, Ill., March 24–28.

Powers, P. J. 1993. *A Comparison of Faculty and Institutional Practices between Teacher Education and the Liberal Arts and Sciences.* ERIC Document Reproduction Service, no. ED 377190.

Project 30 Alliance. 2001. *Updates.* [Online]. Available: *www.project30.org/news.htm.* [8 March 2002].

Reynolds, W. Ann. 1997. What College and University Presidents Can Do to Strengthen Teacher Preparation. In *Strengthening Teacher Education: The Challenges to College and University Leaders,* edited by Peter C. Magrath, Robert L. Egbert, et al. Jossey-Bass Higher Education Series. San Francisco: Jossey-Bass.

Rothenberg, Julia J. 1995. "Pedagogical Seminars in the Arts and Sciences." Paper presented at the Annual Meeting of the American Educational Research Association, San Francisco, Calif., April 18–22. ERIC Document Reproduction Service, ED 387030.

Sokolow, Stephen L. 1997. Teachers for the 21st Century. In *The Superintendents' and Deans' Summit on Transformation and Collaboration for Student Success (April 22–23, 1997) Summary Report.* ERIC Document Reproduction Service, ED 435 775.

Chapter 6

Finding the Third Space: On Leadership Issues Related to the Integration of Library and Computing

CHRIS FERGUSON
Dean for Information Resources, Pacific Lutheran University

and

TERRY METZ
College Librarian & Vice President for Technology and Information Services, Wheaton College

Each year the *sturm und drang* of technology brings library and computing closer together within academe. Distinctions among digital information, electronic pathways, and computer hardware and software on the one hand—and among the various agencies that support these resources on the other hand—are increasingly complex and difficult to negotiate. Many institutions choose to maintain the status quo of separate administrative and operational domains for library and computing, but each year more universities acknowledge the inevitable and bring these centers closer together, seeking new service synergies and less operational overlap.

The world is changing, and so are library and computing organizations. Not so long ago, academic libraries were generally maligned as technological backwaters resistant to change. These days libraries are at the forefront of innovation, delivering real-time information resources and services through the network while working to understand more fully the dynamics of information-seeking in electronic environments. Campus technology agencies, historically regarded as unresponsive to mainstream user needs and perceived as being overly interested in advancing their own vision of a digital future, now typically work closely and responsively with their chief constituencies. In short, libraries are turning the corner in transitioning from a largely print to a largely digital scholarly communication and learning environment, primarily by gaining experience in supporting technology within their own organizations and finding ways to work with technologists across administrative lines. And technology organizations in academe are evolving into service agencies, a metamorphosis due in no small measure to the expanding presence of IT help desks, an increased focus on cultivating a service culture, and closer working relationships with such historically service-oriented agencies as the library.

Computing and library service agencies are in fact morphing into one operation, a phenomenon predicted long ago and for some time chronicled from the front lines of change. (See Seiden and Kathman, 2000, for a thorough survey of the leading contributions to this literature, and Oden et al., 2001 for a more recent case study and bibliography.) As libraries have realized they cannot single-handedly muster all the technologies they need, and as computing organizations realize they cannot adequately address all the service expectations of their clientele, both reach across administrative lines to draw on the expertise and resources of the other. Whether this coming together is due to increased reliance on the network, proliferation of networked resources, scrutiny of service costs and efficiencies, or some combination of these and other factors (Seiden and Kathman, 2000: 10; Ferguson, 2000), it remains clear that the quest for a true understanding of user needs in an electronic age and a concomitant focus on teaching, learning, and research with technology are mutual and compelling interests. These driving forces are characterized by Ferguson (2000) as convergence of information services and information technologies, proliferation of ubiquitous and portable computing, and an evolving service environment. One can readily see library and computing coming still closer together in any number of ways as these service, technology, and fiscal trends continue.

At Pacific Lutheran University (PLU), integration thus far has meant administrative union under a dean, where the initial benefits have been financial flexibility, shared space planning, collaboration on library automation projects, and shared instructional efforts. Building on these successes, PLU is now entering a planning phase that likely will lead to new organizational configurations in support of integrated service environments both on-site and through the network. At Wheaton College integration means the first steps toward mutual support among three sister information units—the library, academic computing, and information technology and services—during the past year. Even during this inaugural year, Wheaton has realized several benefits, including budget flexibility, cooperation in space planning, unified instruction and grant writing efforts, comprehensive student employee training initiatives, joint public relations projects, and greater attention to information needs and services at the highest levels of the institution's administration.

Integration of computing and library organizations is by no means limited to smaller institutions. The University of Southern California (USC) has brought libraries and computing together under a chief information officer, and USC has fully integrated information and technical support services in its Leavey Library information commons. The Anderson School of Business at the University of California, Los Angeles has combined its computing organization with the business library to form a single agency. This agency supports both endeavors, initially separately across administrative units but increasingly through shared resources and an administrative structure that is wholly within neither the University Libraries nor the Anderson School.

Libraries and computing clearly are coming closer together in a variety of ways and in a broad range of institutional settings. Typically, larger-scale associations begin administratively; then at some point common service endeavors break down conventional organization silos. Many units within the former organizations, such as administrative computing and library technical services, can be largely unaffected by an integration. Yet if one recognizes the broad technology and service trends and understands that operational integration in service arenas is an evolutionary process with many variations, the real question on many campuses may no longer be *whether* these organizations become one but rather *when* and *how* they will do so.

For the organization leader, whether technologist or librarian by training, the challenge of this situation becomes less one of seeing some form of integration coming than understanding how best to prepare for or lead an orderly transition from separate agencies into some form of organizational and operational convergence. The leader's true challenge thus becomes one of exercising a kind of leadership that rises above both library and computing cultures and seeks out a third space—somewhere outside both computing and the library as historically defined—into which both organizations can go, at least in part. Much has been written to describe integration efforts, and several authors have prescribed some of the steps needed to get from here to there. This article, however, seeks a deeper understanding of the anthropology of library and computing cultures, explores the imperatives for integration, then discusses some of the leadership qualities and style that are critical to successful integration of two frequently disparate organizations.

AN ANTHROPOLOGY OF THE TRIBES

Survey of cultural differences

Organizational culture—the shared attitudes, values, goals, and practices that characterize work groups—has a significant influence upon the interaction of groups. Libraries and computing units have been perceived as having separate and distinct functions and, thus, belonging to two different organizational cultures (Creth, 1993; Martin, 1992; Ross, 1997; and Woodsworth et al., 1992). Psychologists understand that dividing a large group into two smaller groups causes subjects to cooperate more with in-group members and to show much more competitive behavior with the out-group (Kiesler, 1995: 5). In addition, researchers identify at least three characteristics that further impede collaboration among such groups: (1) social distinctions, (2) compensation differentiation, and (3) subcultural differences (Kiesler, 1995: 5). All of these findings are at play among library and computing work groups, where academic credentials, salary structures, and stature and status in the academic community differ (Woodsworth et al., 1992: 253).

Social distinctions. Technologists do not necessarily share a common professional or academic preparation, nor is it routine for technologists to share a socializing process prior to accepting a position at a college or university. A scholarly pedigree and many years of professional experience generally are not necessary for the new technologist to begin making immediate meaningful contributions to the group's goals and objectives. Technical expertise is highly valued and helps determine salary and status within the peer group (Creth, 1993: 199–121). Librarians, by this measure, may be devalued (Ross, 1997: 132). Academic librarians, who will often align themselves with the more scholarly realm of teaching faculty, may view themselves as being positioned more closely to the parent institution's core mission of teaching, research, and service than their computing colleagues (Creth, 1993: 120).

Compensation differentiation. Wage or salary dispersion negatively affects teamwork and collaboration by reinforcing status and power differences and hierarchy. Greater dispersion creates less willingness to collaborate. Social distinctions between librarians and computing professionals can be reinforced at those colleges and universities that classify these groups into separate job families. Each job family tends to have different salary and responsibility gradations; benefit packages may differ to include, for example, faculty status or sabbaticals for librarians but not for technology professionals. Conversely, compensation among technologists is generally significantly higher than among librarians. Not infrequently, a newly hired campus technologist with three years in the job force may command a greater salary than a professional library manager with decades of experience.

Subcultural differences. Subcultures are useful when they stabilize groups and help people become socialized to a workplace, but they can also increase the distance between groups. Subcultures exist within both the library and computing tribes. Technologists supporting pedagogical efforts have significantly different aims from those supporting administrative tools such as enterprise-wide systems. The priorities and challenges of the hardware specialist do not necessarily coincide with those of the software application support specialist. User services staff in computing organizations face different demands from those of programmers or network technicians. Of course, libraries, too, already have a long history of cultural differences between public services and technical services staff as well as between librarians and support staff (Hirschon, 1998: 9). In addition, a gender dynamic is also present, with the majority of library employees being female and the majority of computing staff still frequently being male.

Different leadership traditions

Hardesty has published widely the results of his interviews with leaders of these organizations (Hardesty, 2000, 1998, 1997, 1997). He found that library directors and computer center administrators generally had dissimilar professional backgrounds. While the library directors all had the same graduate degree—the masters in library science—computer center administrators did not have a common degree. Undergraduate and graduate degrees in the social sciences and humanities predominated among the library directors. Undergraduate and graduate degrees in mathematics and the sciences (both virtually nonexistent among degrees held by library directors) predominated among the computer center administrators, although a few had degrees in the social sciences and the humanities.

Unlike the educational path to becoming a library director, there is no formal educational path to becoming a computer center administrator. Many computer center administrators were once classroom faculty members interested in technology. Ten to fifteen years later, these individuals find themselves overseeing complex and rapidly evolving organizations—challenging to even the best-prepared managers. Computer center administrators have experienced a dramatic growth in their responsibilities, often evolving from heading small operations to heading dynamic units with scores of staff members with disparate backgrounds. Not surprisingly, two sets of individuals with generally quite different preparations for their positions will tend to bring dissimilar perspectives to their responsibilities, making effective communications between the two groups challenging.

Library directors described "service" as a core value of the library profession but not of technologists. Responses by some computer center administrators tended to support the view that the service orientation of the two groups differs. Computer centers are a relatively recent addition to the campus and consequently do not have a long history as stable organizations. The rate of change is incredibly swift in this area. From the computer side, the librarians appear to move more slowly and cautiously. Computer center administrators saw librarians as having many standards from which they could not deviate. They considered libraries as very structure- and tradition-laden.

WHY LIBRARY AND COMPUTING *SHOULD* INTEGRATE

Despite what on the surface may seem insurmountable cultural and operational differences, library and computing professionals have more in common than not, and in the end, both are committed to the same overarching institutional goals. In the early twenty-first century, technology has brought these camps very close together, to the extent that many important activities are common to both libraries and computing operations: designing and using networked resources; collecting and organizing information in multiple formats; creating, maintaining, querying, and managing databases; analyzing user service needs; providing consulting and technical assistance; developing training tools and documentation; and instructing faculty, students, and staff in all of the above (Woodsworth et al., 1992: 252–253). And both organizations face such fundamental challenges as meeting rising user expectations and demands, revamping services and procedures, understanding new technologies, retraining themselves and expanding skill sets, and coping simultaneously with change and the convergence of their responsibilities (Sanders, 1992: 196). Indeed, the goals of each are much the same: helping users to access, manipulate, or use information—in all its definitions—through the optimal use of available tools.

Unlike a decade ago, libraries are no longer the sole information resource on campus, nor are they the only source of access to information. By the same token, campus technology units are neither the only technical resources nor the sole sources of technical support. In many cases, a user does not know whom to ask when confronting an information or technology need. Undoubtedly, our campus communities can benefit from a more coherent and predictable set of channels for dealing with questions and problems (Bly, 1996: 215–216). In addition, libraries and computer centers alike face many thorny policy issues that revolve around information in electronic format, such as freedom of access to information, intellectual property rights, fair use, and site licenses. (Woodsworth, 1988: 23)

There are practical benefits to bringing computing and libraries closer together as well: service improvements and perhaps some service unification, greater organizational flexibility, improved campus visibility on the topic of technology leadership, budget flexibility and leverage, combined strategic planning, and joint research and development. An integrated operation legitimizes and encourages teamwork, and it provides many opportunities for professional growth (Hirschon, 1998: 30).

To ensure that the fortunes of our institutions are enhanced, all components of information services on our campuses must work together closely and intelligently to apply the converging information technologies that underpin our operations. Library and computing staffs have special and complementary skills that are in short supply on our campuses. Working together, these staffs foster mutual respect among work groups, reduce the risk of building information systems designed to operate on railroads of different gauges, and are poised to become a powerful influence on research and scholarship.

FOUNDATION FOR INTEGRATION

An important rule of thumb emerges from the literature on the anthropology and integration of computing and library organizations: All integration is local. Some compelling external forces and the serendipity of opportunity may precipitate a given integration, but when and how they manifest are highly dependent on a variety of local factors, including organization structures and cultures, history, past efforts at collaboration, key personalities, and so on. The models available for integration seem simple on the surface—either a confederation of two organizations administratively joined but operationally separate or a culturally diverse republic that shares delivery of common services while maintaining some sense of individuality. In point of fact, each occurrence of integration represents a point on a continuum rather than membership within a discrete set of homogeneous categories. As noted earlier, within a given instance true integration may occur only in portions of the larger organization with some areas of the organization remaining largely unaffected.

If the highly localized character of integration is a useful rule of thumb, then keen sensitivity to cultural and political nuances is the lesson to be heeded by those who lead integrations. And herein lie the special challenges for the leader of an integration—doing the right things according to the prescriptions and blueprints of the experts, as above, but all the while sensing how these blueprints are best adapted to local needs, sometimes through the invention of new devices.

Local nuances of culture, history, and personality can be demanding for leaders of integration. "The CIO job," writes Hirshon in the context of organizational integration, "is not for the faint of heart" (Hirschon, 1998: 30). Or as Robert Renaud observes in a particularly prescient commentary on computing-library integration:

> In general, the deeper the merger, the higher the benefits to the college but the harder it is to manage the department. Conversely, the more superficial the merger, the lower the gains, but the easier it is to manage. This begins to make sense when we remember that mergers bring very different skills and cultures together. In deep mergers, the mix of staff brought together in new teams brings unexpected insights to problem solving. On the other hand, it requires a high degree of coordination not to run off the rails (Renaud, 2001: 988–989).

Leading an integration can indeed be as physically and emotionally demanding as it can be exhilarating. Yet it is precisely here where the greatest reward of leading a newly formed organization into new territory to do new and better things can be realized—by transcending previous notions of tribe, by fostering a new culture, and by setting into motion ways to sustain a collective vision.

TRANSCENDING TRIBES, MELDING CULTURES

While local circumstances do indeed shape the character and direction of an integration, there remain several overarching factors essential for the formation of a self-aware and self-sustaining integrated organization. These factors, all of which can and should be affected by the leader, include using robust communication and an integrated leadership group to move into a third space beyond library and computing.

Find a third space beyond computing and library. The new organization should be galvanized by a vision and values that draw on the best of both previous organizations, help each to identify with the other, and motivate all to participate in building something new that would not have been likely otherwise. Only in this way is the leadership group likely to be self-aware and self-sufficient for long-term success. Sharrow describes a scenario for cross-boundary collaboration that nonetheless enumerates some of the integrating foci a leader can establish for a new integrated group, beginning with priority setting, communication structures, budget review, and deep understanding of processes (Sharrow, 1995: 55–56).

A still more transforming approach can be to launch a major new initiative that forces several units to reassess their roles within the organization. One such initiative might be the relocation of a computer user room within a library to create an information commons. A dramatic expansion of the number of computers requiring support, broad access to productivity and multimedia development software, and a new kind of environment for seeking and using information forces several units within the organization to rethink how they provide services, which services they in fact ought to provide, and their relationships with other units. Another transforming initiative might be creation of a shared service space or gateway within the network—a common service center that reduces the distinction between library and computing, enables the user to move more intuitively between resources and services, and provides integrated real-time support for research and technology. Here, too, the affected departments must rethink what they do, how they do it, and with whom they must work in new ways. The circumstances created by either of these initiatives provide the transformative moment for the leader of an integrating organization that can be used both to respond to the underlying forces that brought the organizations together and to accelerate the shaping of one that is still more responsive to these trends in the future.

Communication is key. Arguably the most underestimated and yet most powerful dimension of any organizational change, ample and timely communication within all sectors of the organization (and with key individuals and agencies outside the organization), is simply irreplaceable. Those not directly involved in planning or in other leadership roles need to know what is happening and why, and people outside the organization need to know where the organization is going, why it is doing so, and what it will take to move in the directions outlined. Insufficient communication (as gauged by the potential recipient, rather than by the leader) invites alienation and any number of responses, from both inside and outside the organization, that can impede or even prevent success.

On the other hand, an effective program of communication conveys new perspectives and values, gives evidence that much is happening to advance these values, and in a still broader sense lays the foundation for a community with a shared vision and sense of direction. Just how the leader chooses to communicate is largely a local consideration, drawing on some blend of familiar practices and new approaches that in and of themselves signal movement into new common space. Whenever possible, though, the content of the communication should reinforce common values, celebrate diversity, and underscore the melding of cultures. In the case of an information commons in the offing, one might frequently reinforce the desire to support research in an increasingly digital age, the role of reference and help desks in bridging traditional boundaries, and the new culture of integrated information access.

An integrated leadership group is essential. A leader cannot do it all alone (see the Renaud quotation above). Formation and maintenance of a vision powerful enough to overcome the inertia of two cultures is tricky business. Someone with charisma and the power of one or two fetching ideas may be successful in doing so single-handedly in the short run, but in the longer run the cultures will not have melded and the organization's *raison d'être* will not evolve as circumstances change. The appearance of integration will last only as long as the ideas that brought it together. Centrifugal tribal forces will prevail in the end.

Integration truly begins with the formation of a decision-making and planning arena that draws from all sectors of the new organization. This is so not just because it is requisite for the stability and viability of a truly integrated organization, but because "all of us think better than any of us" is a mantra of integration that underscores one of the fundamental reasons for pursuing it in the first place (Bennis and Biederman, 1997: frontispiece). It is precisely this value of collaborative thinking among those with diverse perspectives that provides such large payoffs for integrated approaches to designing and delivering information services, addressing nettlesome policy issues, and coping with the daunting challenges of funding technology.

Forming an effective leadership group as a platform for shared decision making and vision formation—all steeped in robust communication—is an important step toward creating a new organization with a distinctively different character. An important expectation of this group should be to think up a level, to see the world from the perspective of the organizational leader even as that leader thinks up to the level of an administrator outside the organization. In so doing, all parties begin to think above and beyond their respective cultures and begin, however modestly at first, to create a common third space that encourages unconventional thinking and visioning.

Cultivation of a leadership group in most cases requires both ongoing group support and extensive one-on-one mentoring. Just how and to what extent these are undertaken once again is largely a function of local circumstances and personal predilection, though using these opportunities to promote common goals, think up a level, and transcend conventional cultural barriers is an important tool. Certainly this is one of the most important areas of activity for the leader genuinely committed to creating a self-aware, self-sustaining leadership group with the capacity for leading an integrated organization over the long haul. The stakes are simply too high to risk losing even one opportunity for transformation. This transformation process also is potentially the most draining and frustrating portion of the enterprise for the leader, so the ability to pace oneself and maintain perspective in these pursuits is an important requirement.

SUSTAINING THE VISION

Substantial organizational integration is an integral condition for achieving a new vision of information services in a user environment that differentiates less and less between library and computing, as in the case of an information commons or an integrated service environment in the Web. Sometimes the vision comes before organizational change; other times the vision arises from integration. In either case it is important that the organization leader find ways to sustain the visionary life of an integrated organization, rather than simply find ways to play out the leader's ideas. One formula for a holistic approach to leadership, vision, and organization in this circumstance is V.I.B.E.—vision, inspiration, balance, and enjoyment.

Vision is indispensable, but being a visionary leader is not enough. Having a vision is a good start, but the vision must be articulated in meaningful ways and frequently repeated in different forms and forums. In the end a vision must be steeped in the values of the institution, reinforced by those of the new organization, and calibrated with the goals of the larger institution. A leader can do all that for a time with a unilateral vision at the outset of integration, but she or he must move rapidly to broad-based participation in vision formation and implementation or risk the failure that can come when a unilateral vision or the individual loses luster. A leadership group that thinks in third spaces, communicates well, shares the core values of both computing and library, and includes stakeholders in its visioning is far more likely to realize the promise of integration.

Inspiration is an important ingredient for the success of integration. Participants are being asked to give up the tangible and familiar for what to many seems foreign and uncomfortable. Motivation arising from inclusion is critical on all planes of the organization. Failed integrations tend not to be reported in the literature, but at least one such outcome appears to be in large measure due to the imposition of integration without inclusion in planning or buy-in by the participants (Wagner, 2000). Seeking to create motivation from inclusion also means finding the optimal balance between leadership and participation, which in turn may demand flexibility on the part of the leader in crafting and implementing an integration plan.

Balance is easy to say but difficult to achieve. As with other aspects of leadership for integration, though, it is both important and multifaceted. As a guiding principle for leadership style, the leader must constantly seek the optimal balance between leadership and participation in both the ideational and operational realms. How the leadership group works with the leader, how the leader and leadership group together relate to the larger organization and its constituents, and how these relationships play out in allocation of resources, planning, and the like are aspects of finding a balance between leadership and participation. Equally important is the need to maintain balance in one's personal life, committing to the institution and the ideals of integration, understanding that the early phases of integration especially are physically and emotionally demanding, but over the long term maintaining sources of personal revitalization and growth that keep one's life balanced between professional and personal to the benefit of both. This is just as relevant a principle for the leader as for other participants in the integration effort.

Enjoyment, or just plain fun, is often overlooked as an important ingredient in the leadership formula, especially in a setting with such high stakes as organizational integration. As with balance, enjoyment is absolutely essential for all participants to be healthy both physically and mentally. Laughter is one of the best palliatives for a difficult situation, and general encouragement to enjoy one's work is best inspired by example. Have fun, enjoy your work, and give everyone the freedom to do so in some unconventional ways. There always are limits, but one might be surprised at the extent to which encouragement to have fun can lead to improved morale and increased capacity for thinking differently about the work and the workplace.

CLOSING THOUGHTS

Computing and library organizations have changed considerably in recent years, both adapting to and driven by information technology, contemporary service expectations, and systemic changes underway within higher education generally. Libraries are becoming more like computing centers and computing centers are morphing into something more akin to libraries. Both are gaining a new sense of self and purpose in integrated organizations, even though the definition of those integrated organizations varies considerably from setting to setting.

The network—and by extension, networked resources and services—has been the single most significant force in breaking down previous notions of library and computing. This transforming effect of technology has simultaneously wreaked chaos and permitted exciting new combinations and concentrations of information services and technologies that draw from both the library and the computing arenas. It is the institution with an integrated information services organization that stands to take full advantage of these opportunities. Every year more universities make the commitment to rise above existing cultural differences and organizational barriers to better serve students, faculty, and others who work in an increasingly challenging environment. In the end it is about teaching and learning in an increasingly technological era, rather than inherited notions of library or computing organizations.

These are, to say the least, challenging trends for the information services leader, whether associated with library, computing, or both. Organization cultures, perceptions, and stereotypes and the vicissitudes of local history and personalities add a degree of complexity to operational realities that discourage some institutions from embracing integration and some leaders from stepping forward to advance the principles of integration.

For those who do make the commitment, communication, integrated leadership, and concerted efforts to find a third space for the new organization are key to building a lasting foundation for the integration of library and computing. Vision, inspiration, balance, and enjoyment can be adhering and stimulating forces for a new entity. It is possible to integrate two cultures with such a predisposition for misunderstanding and to forge them in humane fashion into something greater than either would be capable of separately.

Indeed, it is imperative that we do so.

REFERENCES

Beagle, D. 1999. "Conceptualizing an Information Commons." *Journal of Academic Librarianship* 25, no. 2 (March): 82–89.

Bennis, W. and P. W. Biederman. 1997. *Organizing Genius: The Secrets of Creative Collaboration*. Reading, Mass.: Addison-Wesley.

Bly, O. 1996. "Academic Libraries, Academic Computer Centers, and Information Technology." *Advances in Library Administration and Organization*, 14, no. 4: 215–216.

Creth, S. D. 1993. "Creating a Virtual Information Organization: Collaborative Arrangements Between Libraries and Computing Centers." *Journal of Library Administration* 19, no. 3–4: 118–121.

Ferguson, C. 2000. "'Shaking the Conceptual Foundations,' Too: Integrating Research and Technology Support for the Next Generation of Information Service." *College & Research Libraries* 61, no. 4 (July): 300–311.

Hardesty, Larry L. 1997a. "Libraries and Computer Center Relations at Smaller Academic Institutions." *Library Issues* 18 (September): n.p.

———. 1997b. "Relationships between Libraries and Computer Centers at Liberal Arts Colleges." *Research Briefs* 2 (November). Chicago: Council on Library and Information Resources. (Also available online: www.clir.org/pubs/research/rb2.html. [March 2002]).

———. 1998. "Computer Center—Library Relations at Small Institutions: A Look at Both Sides." *Cause/Effect* 21, no. 1 (Spring): 35–41.

———. 2000. Computer Center and Library Relations at Small Colleges. In *Books, Bytes, and Bridges: Libraries and Computer Centers in Academic Institutions*, by L. Hardesty. Chicago: American Library Association: 73–82.

Hirshon, Arnold. 1998. *Integrating Computer Services and Library Services*. CAUSE Professional Papers, 18. Boulder, Colo.: CAUSE.

Kiesler, S. 1995. Working Together Apart. In *Building Partnerships: Computing and Library Professionals. Proceedings of Library Solutions Institute No. 3*, Chicago, Ill., May 12–14, 1994, edited by A. G. Lipow and S. D. Creth. Berkeley, Calif.: Library Solutions Press.

Martin, M. J. 1992. "Academic Libraries and Computing Centers: Opportunities for Leadership." *Library Administration and Management* 14, no. 4 (Spring): 78–79.

Oden, R. A., D. B. Temple, J. R. Cotrell, R. K. Griggs, G. W. Turney, and F. M. Wojcik. 2001. "Merging Library and Computing Services at Kenyon College: A Progress Report." *Educause Quarterly* 24, no. 4: 18–25.

Renaud, Robert. 2001. "What Happened to the Library: When the Library and the Computer Center Merge." *College and Research Libraries News* 62, no. 10 (November): 987–989.

Ross, J. G. 1997. "Defining the Divide: Causes of Friction between Librarians and Computer Support Staff." *Journal of Academic Librarianship* 23, no. 2 (March): 132–133.

Sanders, W. H. 1992. Libraries and Computing Centers: A Marriage in the Making? In *3rd Library and Information Technology Association National Conference*, Denver, Colo. Chicago: American Library Association.

Seiden, P., and M. D. Kathman, 2000. A History of the Rhetoric and Reality of Library and Computing Relationships. Pp. 1–12 in *Books, Bytes, and Bridges: Libraries and Computer Centers in Academic Institutions,* edited by L. Hardesty. Chicago: American Library Association.

Sharrow, M. J. 1995. "Library and IT Collaboration Projects: Nine Challenges." *CAUSE/Effect* 18, no. 4 (Winter): 55–56.

Wagner, R. 2000. "The Gettysburg Experience." Pp. 164–177 in *Books, Bytes, and Bridges: Libraries and Computer Centers in Academic Institutions,* edited by L. Hardesty. Chicago: American Library Association.

Woodsworth, A. 1988. "Computing Centers and Libraries as Cohorts: Exploiting Mutual Strengths." *Journal of Library Administration* 9, no. 4: 21–34.

Woodsworth, A., T. Maylone, and M. Sywak. 1992. "The Information Job Family: Results of an Exploratory Study." *Library Trends* 41, no. 2 (Fall): 250–268.

Part III

Surveying Real-Life Applications

Chapter 7

Transforming Technology Training: Partnerships, Packages, and Policies: The Lone Ranger Doesn't Work Here Any More!

PATTIE ORR
Director of User Services and Computer Science Lecturer, Wellesley College

TRANSFORMING TECHNOLOGY TRAINING: PARTNERSHIPS, PACKAGES, AND POLICIES

For those of us who have been in the information technology (IT) field for a decade or two, thinking back about our approach to training and support will bring back visions of the Lone Ranger. "Hi Ho, Silver!" We were daring and resourceful masked riders leading the fight for law and order in the early cyberwest. We were heroes . . . large and in charge . . . sincere . . . and most of the time, but not always, helpful. Users were at our mercy to give them privileges on our cryptic mainframe systems. When computing was a new frontier, that was probably a necessary approach. Computing is no longer a new frontier, but unfortunately, things have not changed that much in many IT organizations.

We still like to call the shots! We are hesitant to ask for help, join up with a partner, or embrace anything that was "not invented here." We want to help users but are often overwhelmed with the requests for help and training as users begin to really use the technology we have been trying to sell them all of these years. We distance ourselves from the user in order to cope with increasing demand. We fall short of donning the Lone Ranger's mask, but we do try to hide our faces.

As we began to assess the state of training for technology at Wellesley College, we realized we were doing our best, yet not succeeding. We were sincere Lone Rangers, but we could not save the day. In spite of great marketing and hard work, our classes were not meeting the needs of our constituents. After all, even the Lone Ranger had a partner. We needed Tonto! We were fresh out of silver bullets and were going to need some help. We needed partnerships.

How can technology training be transformed on a college campus? Can the power of the Web, networking, and distributed learning strategies provide effective just-in-time training for staff, faculty, and students? What techniques used by commercial vendors or Internet service providers can be implemented on campuses of varying sizes and varying financial or technological means? Can colleagues really team up with new partners to forge new paths for training? What policies will be necessary to implement these new approaches to training?

These were just a few of the questions explored by Wellesley College when we began to investigate what would be needed to transform our ailing software and technology training programs. We knew what challenges we had to meet: effectively meeting diverse training and documentation needs of college community members, keeping up with new software versions, aligning training to meet the individual needs of end users and the work of departments, and providing just-in-time, cost-effective solutions. We had to strategize several options that would fit our campus. As part of my Frye Leadership Institute practicum project in the summer of 2000, I began to redesign technology training at Wellesley College to take advantage of partnerships, packages, and new technology tools. We wanted to provide more personalized, "Just for Me" user support for the Wellesley College community by offering Web-based training, expanding the peer-tutoring support model for students, and developing a "Deskside Coaching" support model for administrators and faculty. This chapter will examine the partnerships formed, policies created, and packages purchased in order to transform training at Wellesley College. It is my sincere hope that the lessons learned can assist other colleagues who desire to redesign software and technology training programs.

TECHNOLOGY AND CHANGE IN HIGHER EDUCATION

Dramatic changes have occurred in the way that the world uses computers for communication, problem solving, and publishing. Use of the Internet has exploded in the past few years and continues to grow exponentially. Changes in computer use, particularly because of extensive campus networking and the expanding World Wide Web, have increasingly become integral parts of teaching, learning, and communicating in higher education.

Wellesley College is a four-year undergraduate liberal arts women's college. Established in 1875, the mission of Wellesley College is to provide an excellent education for women who will make a difference in the world. The student body is composed of 2300 exceptionally bright students. Within our student body, 45 percent are ethnically diverse, 7 percent are international students, and 4 percent are nontraditionally aged students. Most—94 percent—Wellesley students live on-campus.

Students at Wellesley, like most other American college students, are "wired" to the max. In the fall of 2001, 90 percent of the first year students arrived with computers of their own. Laptops comprised 70 percent of the computers brought, giving the incoming class more computing mobility than ever. Since 1994, Wellesley has offered a port for every pillow. Virtually every student who has a computer connects to the network in the dorm. Students often use their laptops in ports provided in the library and other public locations. Students can work wherever they feel most productive and comfortable because they can access the needed tools in the classroom, dorm room, or library.

All students use e-mail and online conferences to communicate and surf our campus-wide information system and the

Internet. Because networking and computer access is easy and ubiquitous at Wellesley, sharing documents, access to syllabi, electronic discussions to support course work, and research on the Internet are all universal. Students use electronic drop boxes to submit work, and electronic online conferences provide access to all sorts of digital resources. Students can conveniently access digitized images, audio files, and video files stored on file servers.

Faculty and staff at Wellesley are also heavy-duty users of technology. All faculty and staff at Wellesley have e-mail access and networked desktop computers with the exception of a few staff in positions within food service, custodial, or craft areas. These employees have e-mail accounts and can use computers as needed within public access areas. Wellesley has many technology-equipped classrooms, and learning has been transformed by the availability of digitized information resources. Faculty use course-centered Web pages, electronic conferences, interactive assignments delivered via the Internet, multimedia instructional tools, and videoconferencing. This effective use of technology has provided an expanded variety of ways for students to be engaged with the material; over 75 percent of the fall 2001 courses incorporated the use of electronic information: approximately 200 courses maintain Web sites on the college-wide Information System, while 295 courses have electronic conferences to allow threaded discussions, chats, and file exchange. Faculty members begin to contact students by e-mail during orientation week. Computing and e-mail are everywhere at Wellesley.

CHALLENGES FOR TRAINING PROGRAMS IN HIGHER EDUCATION

With all of this access, people often say, "Doesn't almost everyone have lots of computer experience? Why would it be necessary to train them to use computing? Aren't things just getting easier and easier?" While it is true that user interfaces are improving in most software, there is still a need for user instruction. Some training challenges facing colleges and universities are:

- Providing high quality, cost-effective training that can foster end user independence;
- Developing a variety of training programs that meet the diverse technology needs of students, staff, and faculty;
- Keeping up to date with the many new versions of software and courseware;
- Addressing security issues, such as virus threats and operating system update requirements;
- Providing documentation to supplement often cryptic help files;
- Closely aligning training programs to the work of departments, campus communities, and the individual needs of end users;
- Providing on-demand and just-in-time training to increase productivity, understanding of software applications, knowledge of the Internet, and Web design.

IT groups want to provide high quality, timely training for their users to empower them to make the most of the information resources the college has to offer. Software training is needed to support academic instruction: students need to know how to format papers, create spreadsheets and charts, scan or create images, and create Web sites or portfolios. Staff members need proficiency in productivity software to complete projects efficiently, and many users need to be able to design Web sites and publish information in HTML. A training program that teaches only software applications is not adequate. College community members need to be "information literate" in order to search for and critically evaluate information sources. User instruction in acceptable use of electronic resources is critically important to creating this "information literate" community.

WHY TRADITIONAL TRAINING PROGRAMS DO NOT WORK

When computing was new, lots of people felt the need to attend classes to figure out these newfangled computers. It was a heyday for trainers. We were in control! The trainer was the expert, and users made it a priority to get this valuable instruction. Applications were cryptic and tricky. Who could ever forget the three-tiered keyboard templates for WordPerfect? In the late 1990s we began to realize our training programs were no longer as successful as they had been before. Undergraduates signed up for classes in droves at the beginning of the semester, but as the demands of "for-credit" courses increased, a technology training class "because someday you are going to need this information" seemed unimportant. Attendance was dropping off for faculty, staff, and students. Even though users rated our classes highly, they signed up less or often cancelled at the last minute.

The levels of expertise within the community were diverse. The previous generic classes for introductory, intermediate, and advanced levels just did not work for people anymore. They often told us that they only needed one small part of the class. They wanted more individual help. In a diverse population such as a college or university, it is a concern that minority students or employees, and first-generation college students would be less likely to come from homes with regular Internet access. This causes a disparity in the computing experience and information fluency among students and employees.

Smaller schools in particular have a hard time offering an adequate number of sessions at the varying levels needed to make training convenient and timely for users. A further complication in recent years is a shortage of qualified IT professionals in colleges that cannot compete with dot-com salary structures. In an environment of understaffing and much turnover, necessary work gets done, but training is often shortchanged. In smaller schools, training is always collateral duty, and there is no IT training director watching out for the overall goals of the program.

Rapid change in software has required more specialization for the professional IT staff, an especially difficult challenge for small IT departments. Budgets for training IT staff are usually very limited in higher education compared with IT staff in business. The cost of outside training can be exorbitant, and support for such extensive retooling is needed from senior staff and human resources.

Lack of standards for software and hardware make it hard

to offer consistent training: inconsistent policies for hardware and software replacement mean that the staff must support and teach many different levels of a product. If hardware does not remain up to date, a portion of the community cannot move forward to the latest and greatest software. The pennywise method of trickling down older computers to those lowest on the academic food chain is disastrous for support. Not only does it cost to do the hardware repairs; the cost of staff time for troubleshooting and the need to support older software and operating systems is terribly expensive. Rising costs of software also make it hard to keep software versions current.

PARTNERSHIPS

Who could help us in our effort to redesign our training? Over the past two years, the Wellesley College User Services Department has developed several critical partnerships. Some were local and others involved relationships beyond campus such as vendors and consortia. Although we would have described ourselves previously as collaborative, it was surprising how many valuable partnerships we had not taken advantage of in the past. Our isolationist Lone Ranger approach was not working, so we moved full steam ahead toward forming partnerships.

The partnership power of consortia

The idea of a consortial approach to higher education is not new. A number of organizations and institutions seek to combine forces to purchase goods and services at reduced rates. Wellesley College belongs to the Boston Consortium (*www.boston-consortium.org*), which goes a step further in this process. The Boston Consortium for Higher Education (TBC), established in 1996 by chief financial officers from Boston-area four-year private colleges and universities, is a diverse group of 13 Boston-area educational institutions: Babson College, Bentley College, Berklee College of Music, Boston College, Boston University, Brandeis University, Harvard University, Massachusetts Institute of Technology, Northeastern University, Olin College, Tufts University, Wellesley College, and Wheaton College. TBC seeks to develop and implement innovative cost management and quality improvement ideas among its member schools.

The Boston Consortium brings together leaders and managers from nonacademic functions to explore similar interests and concerns, to reduce costs, and improve the ongoing operations on their campuses. Fifteen different groups of administrative professionals have been established to allow participants to share best practices and embrace sharing in order to motivate each group to excel. Examples of the types of groups are: Human Resources, Environmental Health and Safety, CFOs, CIOs, Benefits, Employment Managers, Health Services, Risk Management, Bursars, Organizational Development and Training, and an IT Training Group.

The IT Training Group (ITTG) was established in 1998. Representing Wellesley, I began to attend monthly meetings of this group and learned the value of the consortium. My new partners in ITTG freely shared their experiences. It did not take long to realize that we were experiencing common trends. In this informal peer-to-peer setting, we began to discuss ways to collaborate, share training classes, purchase classroom training sessions as a group, and generally to improve our training programs. As we began to get acquainted, relationships in the group provided trust and a foundation for collaborative work. After our initial "getting to know you" sharing phase, the ITTG completed a formal needs assessment to identify common concerns, evaluate opportunities, and facilitate discussion.

One need we identified immediately was that it was hard to provide enough sections of training courses at each campus, and it was challenging to manage contractual arrangements for training provided by outside vendors. The number of courses needed by our users was increasing, and because of the difficulty in filling IT staff positions, it was hard to provide quality training. Contracting for vendor provided training was expensive, and smaller schools had very little recourse if the quality of training was poor.

As a group the consortium serves 45,000 employees and 122,000 students. There is strength in numbers. TBC schools annually outsourced 35 percent of all IT training, and the combined annual spending on outsourced training was $400,000, but all consortium members struggled to fill all of their training seats. Members estimated that on average, two to nine seats were unfilled in each training class; that is, approximately 9,400 seats per year across the consortium representing a lost opportunity cost of approximately $94,000 per year. How could this be improved? What could be done? Armed with a better understanding of each other's programs and needs we began to look for solutions.

SOLUTION STRATEGIES DEVELOPED BY ITTG

ITTG members began to post unfilled seats in courses to a central electronic mailing list. This allowed training directors at other institutions to offer classes or seminars to their users. This was done without additional charge among consortium-member institutions. Offering this opportunity helped to make use of seats that would have otherwise gone empty and helped all schools offer a variety of courses more frequently than before. Schools that could offer the open seats did so; smaller schools that had fewer open seats to offer contributed to the group in other ways, such as hosting consortium meetings or training events. It was sort of a fuzzy quid pro quo, but it worked well and most likely could never have been accomplished if we worked through a pure charge-back model. Everyone was delighted with the outcome.

Select preferred vendors for classroom-based training

The goals for this project were to:

- Provide up-to-date, high quality training in a variety of subject areas;
- Negotiate favorable pricing for TBC schools;
- Identify vendors who would work with ITTG to develop mutually beneficial opportunities;
- Increase vendors' understanding of higher education training needs so that they could provide better-customized services.

Each school suggested vendors it had used in the past, and ITTG established criteria for rating vendors (see Figure 1). After extensive interviews, site visits, and teaching demonstrations, five vendors were selected, and we created the *IT Higher Education Learning Partnership* (IT HELP). Two vendors were awarded "top tier" status because of the depth and breadth of their class offerings and their flexible pricing arrangements. Three other vendors were given second tier status and were used minimally to provide training if the two preferred vendors could not meet our needs. Between July 1, 1999, and December 31, 2001, the 12 schools that participated in the IT HELP program spent cumulatively $688,503, on training programs with the two "top tier" vendors. Without the consortial agreement, the cost for this training would have been $1.2 million. Cumulative savings during this period was $550,003, which represents a 44 percent reduction of costs as a result of the leverage of the collective buying power of the schools.

Evaluate and select a preferred vendor for Web-based training

A problem identified by each school was the need to offer more personalized "just-in-time" training for users. We all needed to be able to offer on-demand training that was not time bound. Although there were several Web-based products on the market for such purposes, the cost was exorbitant. A number of the products were really just retrofitted CD-based courses now offered with Web front-ends. The files were very large and needed to be hosted locally; accessing the files from the vendor across the Internet would have produced performance and bandwidth issues.

We were looking for a Web-based product that:

- Offered large numbers of high quality software titles;
- Was written for the Web and was broken into small links to maximize bandwidth;
- Would run on both Macintosh and PCs;
- Would run effectively on a 56K or better modem;
- Offered 24/7, high quality technical support;

Figure 1
Preferred Vendor Rating Criteria Classroom-Based Training

INSTRUCTOR-LED TRAINING

Depth of PC offerings
Depth of Mac offerings
Depth of technical offerings
Open enrollment PC offerings
Open enrollment Mac offerings
Open enrollment technical offerings
Quality of courseware
Quality of instructors
Ability to offer LearnPro style class

PRICING FOR INSTRUCTORS

Overall price competitiveness
Options/flexibility for 1/2 day pricing

RELATED SERVICES

Web-based training
Follow-up phone support
Web-based registration
Skills assessment
Marketing of schedule
Custom documentation services
Computer-based training
Certified testing center facilities

VENDOR TRAINING SITES

Appearance/organization
Refreshments
Parking
Quantity/diversity
Accessibility of public transportation

OPERATIONS

Knowledge of/experience with higher education
Retention of account reps
Willingness to do work with other vendors
Ability to handle high request volume
Merger/acquisition potential

- Could easily produce reports;
- Made system administration simple.

Each of us hoped a product would be out there that would meet our needs, but doing a thorough product evaluation alone seemed like a daunting task. And even if we found a product that seemed appropriate, would it be so expensive that most schools would only be able to offer it to a few users? This seemed like a perfect collaborative project.

In the fall of 1999, the ITTG sent out a request for information to several Web-based training vendors (see Figure 2). Seven companies answered our request and were rated according to the criteria we had established as a group.

Three products were chosen by the ITTG for testing. We felt the best way to test the products was to get a group of users from each school and actually use trial accounts (see Figure 3). We agreed that we would ask five to seven users from each school to participate in an all-day event at the MIT Professional Learning Center. Users were asked to select one software product and to try the lessons from all three of the vendors. Evaluation forms were set up on the consortium Web site. After one month of trying the products at home, the testers were asked to submit answers to the same evaluation questions again. A successful agreement was reached for the top-ranked product, basing the pricing on anticipated levels of participation.

Working together, we formed a true partnership with the vendor as we trained our system administrators together, planned roll-out strategies, and shared documentation. Working together to roll out the product was effective and lightened the load on all participants. We had accomplished with our partners what would have been difficult or impossible for Wellesley to do alone, and we had done so at a reduced cost.

PARTNERSHIPS FOR PROFESSIONAL DEVELOPMENT AND LICENSING

Another extraordinarily helpful partnership is Wellesley's association with NERCOMP (North East Regional Computing, www.nercomp.org), a regional affiliate of EDUCAUSE (www.

Figure 2
Web-Based Training Request for Information

A. Company Information
- 1. Who is your parent company?
- 2. Who is involved in your instructional design team?
- 3a. What sort of customer support do you provide?
- 3b. Do you offer first-line customer support?
- 4. Would we be able to log onto your server, or is yours a LAN-based product only?
- 5. What technology(ies) do you use to write the programs?
- 6. What's your Internet architecture?
- 7. Does your company provide technology training only? If no, what other types of training do you offer?

B. Product Requirements
- 1a. Do we need plug-ins to use your program?
- 1b. If yes, which ones, and how are they obtained?
- 2. What are the browser requirements for using your Web-based training product? Does your product require a specific browser?
- 3. Can end users download your training, or do they need to do it online?
- 4. Will users be able to access your site/courses from both their office and their home?

C. Special Features
- 1. Do you have online skills assessments?
- 2. Do you have pre- and post-course testing?
- 3. Does your product bookmark where users have stopped in any given course, or do users need to start from the beginning if they are unable to finish a course in one sitting?
- 4. Do you provide a "learn and try" environment (i.e., can one learn about an application and then try the actual application, or a very close Web-based simulation)?
- 5. Do you incorporate human interaction into your programs (e.g., a mentoring system, peer-to-peer chats)?
- 6a. Do you offer other features like online documentation?
- 6b. If yes, can the user easily print your documentation?
- 6c. Do you provide printable file formats?

Figure 2 *(Continued)*
Web-Based Training Request for Information

D. Licensing
  1. Are your courses available on CD-ROM as well as being Web-based?
  2. What are all your media options? How do they affect pricing?
  3. Is the licensing you offer concurrent or per individual?
  4. How frequently do you update your site?
  5a. How often do you update the course material?
  5b. When are updates done?
  5c. When updates are done, how do they affect students who are in the middle of courses being updated?

Please note briefly any special or unique features you feel your product offers.

educause.edu). NERCOMP offers collaboration opportunities in many different areas, but the opportunity for our IT staff to attend Special Interest Group (SIG) meetings on various topics of interest for professional development has been especially helpful. The value of training and connections with other IT professionals in the northeast cannot simply be measured quantitatively. It has been a lifesaver for our staff! SIGs have been held on many topics including Helpdesk Management, Virus Management, Network Topics, Instructional Strategies, Web Site Development, and ADA Compliance in Computing.

The NERCOMP connection has helped us take advantage of consortial pricing and negotiation for site licensing for virus software and productivity software. The low pricing helps us keep our software versions in sync, ultimately permitting us to offer a much more effective and efficient training program. Realizing the effectiveness of such regional consortia, EDUCAUSE is exploring other such relationships around the country. At present, in addition to NERCOMP, there are the EDUCAUSE Mid-Atlantic, EduTex, NWACC/EDUCAUSE (Northwest Academic Computing Conference), and the EDUCAUSE SouthEast Regional groups.

Figure 3
Evaluation Questions for Web-Based Training

Which vendor did you test?

Which platform did you use?

Which program did you test?

How easy was it to navigate through this vendor's Web-based training (10=very easy, 1=very difficult)?

How relevant was the content of this course to your ability to learn this program (10=very relevant, 1=not relevant)?

How well did the course keep you engaged (10=very engaging, 1=boring)?

Was it easy to get help? If you didn't use help, did it appear easy to access?

If this vendor's Web-based training were offered at your campus, would you make use of it?

Would you recommend this training program to a colleague?

Was there anything that really stood out for you about this program . . . a great plus, or perhaps a very unfortunate aspect?

If you tested this program in more than one sitting, was there a bookmarking feature that you used?

- Yes, and it was easy to use
- Yes, but not easy to use
- I could have used a bookmark option but didn't see it
- I tested the program in one sitting so I didn't notice.

Overall, how would you rank this vendor's product (10=highest rating, 1=poorest rating)?

LOCAL PARTNERSHIPS ARE OFTEN OVERLOOKED

It seems odd that IT staff are usually open to the idea of partnership with IT staff from other colleges or universities, while overlooking the value of partnerships within their own college or university. Maybe it was the nature of the Internet and our listserv heritage. While we value getting help from other IT professionals and sharing expertise, these homogeneous, in-house partnerships with others in IT do not offer us the benefits of heterogeneous alliances. It seemed that achieving successful collaboration with staff in non-technical areas was often a mystery to us. To achieve true institutional improvement for our training programs at Wellesley, though, a variety of partnerships would be necessary.

For me, the most valuable aspect of the Frye Institute was the way that the program helped me to understand the perspective of the various stakeholders in the college setting. The very first assignment for the Frye Institute was to conduct an interview with a few of the leaders on our campus. I chose to interview our Vice President of Information Services, an Associate Dean of the College, our Chief Financial Officer (CFO), the Deputy Director of Human Resources, the Vice President for Administration and Planning, and the Registrar. Using the questions below, I began to see how they approached IT issues and to understand a little about their own decision-making style.

- How are you and your department changing approaches to gathering and using information? Is the use of digital information increasing?
- How has information technology changed your work/teaching/learning/research/publishing?
- What new kinds of support services do you need? Is there a plan to meet those needs?
- Do you and your staff have the necessary skills to use information technology? How are you gaining those skills? What does the campus need to do to be sure that staff, faculty, and students are kept abreast of information technology developments?
- How are priorities and associated budgets set? Have you

seen changes in budgeting and priorities as a result of information technology?

- What are your frustrations and fears regarding technology?
- How would you like to see our training efforts change on campus for information technology support?
- What is your view on the direction of information technology on campus? What is it? What will it be? What should it be? What problems need to be addressed?

I had not previously had much opportunity to meet individually with these leaders. These conversations confirmed my understanding of the importance of their buy-in to any program that might successfully change support practices at Wellesley.

After the Frye Institute concluded, I contacted each person on my list for a follow-up meeting to tell them about my experience and my plan to redesign our technology training program implementing a Web-based training solution. I needed to gain support collegewide for the project and to persuade the decision makers to provide significant funding for the training contract. Since our budget had no previous line for such outsourced training, this was going to be a challenge.

To my delight, when I returned and asked for the follow-up meetings, each person welcomed the opportunity, and the proposal improved with each discussion. In fact, the CFO helped me to gather up end-of-year money to provide for our Web-based training.

One of the most useful partnerships that I developed was with our Human Resources (HR) Department, which was interested in our technology training for employees as part of the "Valuing Work @ Wellesley" initiative. The HR Department was leading a redesign project to create a flexible compensation program that not only focused on the skills and behaviors valued at Wellesley College but also provided a baseline for an effective performance evaluation and reward system. Work roles were being redefined and would more accurately represent the technology requirements of the positions. Human Resources was open to and interested in new approaches for offering both technology training and information resource instruction. They invited us to speak to the Administrative Council about the initiative, helped us contact all department supervisors, and listed the new training license as one of the HR employee benefits on their Web page. We could not have asked for more support.

Another valuable connection was our relationship with the Wellesley College Library. Wellesley has a merged Library/IT organization called Information Services (IS). All of the traditional IT areas and the library jointly report to the Vice President of Information Services and College Librarian. The library has a long history of strong user-instruction programs and of promoting electronic information resources. We worked together to roll out the new online product, and our Digital Library Specialist serves as the primary system administrator. As partners we promoted the use of the new product throughout our organization.

In order to promote the product to faculty and students, we developed several academic partnerships. The Dean of Students was extremely supportive and invited us to promote the new initiative at the Fall New Faculty Orientation. He also gave me a list of faculty who used technology heavily in instruction. I could call upon them and set up a demonstration of the product. This was quite a "calling card" to help reach out to faculty. We demonstrated the product to faculty and agreed to do "study breaks" for their classes to show their students how to use it. Faculty members who require students to use products like Excel, Word, PowerPoint, Dreamweaver, or Photoshop in their classes do not want to "teach" the software. They want to teach their subjects. It was very successful to partner with the faculty to demonstrate the online training product to their students so those students could "self-serve" instruction on demand. We took advantage of opportunities to make presentations to the faculty at Learning and Teaching Center events and faculty workshops.

There were several ways that we promoted the online training product to students. Instructions on using the Web-based training were distributed at orientation to all incoming students. The student consultants and tutors were asked to use and promote the product to students in labs, dorms, and tutoring sessions. We have found that the online software training approach works well for students because of its 24/7 availability. Students are generally nocturnal, and their available hours never matched the hours that IT staff could offer classes and demonstrations.

The Internet culture has made our society very interested in services that are customized and instantly available 24/7. Popular Internet shopping sites use "cookies" to remember the shopping and surfing habits of customers; many offer online chat for assistance and are available 365 days a year, 24 hours a day. This is the type of support and training that our college students have come to expect, and partnering with our vendor has allowed us to offer this to our constituents. The vendor hosts the site and help is available 24/7 for our constituents by e-mail, chat, threaded discussion, or phone.

To fully integrate the new training product into our entire college community, we needed to abolish the old ineffective training classes and ease our community into a new system of training and support. We were able to come up with several methods to introduce and maintain the new product (see Appendix).

PUTTING POLICIES INTO PLACE

Technology is really very easy . . . it's the people who are hard! To an IT professional, the idea of transforming our training program was primarily about choosing good training strategies, setting up accounts for a Web-based training product, and marketing those new ideas. It is the policy that surrounds any transformational initiative, however, that is most likely to be a stumbling block. When designing our new training program at Wellesley, there were three basic policy questions.

Policy Question 1: Who will be included in the new Web-based training program?

Most Web-based training is purchased on an individual license basis. Since the programs collect the data for each individual on the lessons completed and the scores for assessments, it is not feasible to share licenses. The power of a Web-based training tool is the individualization. In higher education we were accustomed to the idea of concurrent use. This is not the strategy for licensing Web-based software, nor would it be effective. Since each license costs, schools have to decide who will be given this benefit. Will it be just faculty? Will it be faculty and administrative staff? What about union members, non-exempt employees, and staff who do not have a computer on their desk? What about students?

At Wellesley we paired the transformation of our technology training program with the new "Valuing Work @ Wellesley" initiative from the Human Resources Department. This initiative supported a strong sense of purpose and mission for professional development. Technology was a part of this development, and we wanted all Wellesley employees to have the opportunity. Even employees in jobs that did not use a computer were given the opportunity to have a license for the Web-based training. This would allow them the opportunity to work to develop technology skills on their own time, which might help prepare them for higher-level jobs in their own department or across the college. All faculty, staff, and students were given the opportunity to take advantage of a license for Web-based training at Wellesley. Clearly, not everyone will take this opportunity, but the new policy opened the door equally for all.

Policy Question 2: With Web-based training, users can train 24/7, so how much work time will be allocated to the employee for training?

In our old model for training, employees were given time away from their desks to attend workshops and software training classes. When rolling out our new initiative, we urged managers to be sure to plan training time for the staff. In some positions it would be possible to train at the desk during slow periods. In other jobs, that would be impossible. It is expected that at least some training happens on the clock. It is true that many employees do train outside of work hours, and for certain situations, that is appropriate. However, managers need to make an appropriate allocation of regularly scheduled time for training. Getting a quality product for training is easy; getting people to make time to train and managers to release employees to do so is more difficult. The HR Director and the Dean of the College wanted to be sure that employees and their managers knew that they should work together to set goals for training. To assist in this planning, we held multiple demonstrations of the new system and invited all employees to feel free to use our public labs for training. Students are in class during the day, and there are adequate public computers to accommodate employees who need a place to work. We also held "Open Lab" sessions on certain days and advertised that a staff member was on duty in a particular lab. If employees wanted a quiet place to train or help getting started, they could stop by.

Policy Question 3: Who will be allowed to see the user data from the Web-based training?

This was the most challenging policy question. Employees in our test group were very concerned about this question. They were afraid their managers would see the time spent on lessons and think they were spending "too much time" on training. Many feared that their managers would use the scores they made on assessments against them in promotion decisions. Some employees wanted to work on their own time to learn technology in hopes of someday qualifying for a different job, possibly out of the department where they presently work. Being an organization that wants to promote learning, we chose to implement a policy that is similar to our policy for library records. In collaboration with our HR Director and the senior staff of the college, we decided that we would report only aggregate data. We would not report individual data. This is similar to the privacy that an employee is given for a library record. I believe this decision was a crucial turning point for the project. Users want to explore, dabble, and learn. They can print out their own transcript or print certificates to authenticate their scores for their manager if that is needed. Handling the data in this way put the control in the hands of the employee. As an administrator for the system, I have seen that most use the program by jumping around. After all, most of our employees would not need to do an entire Excel module. They just need the parts they do not know. Or they just need to refresh themselves on something they have done before. Doing a module from start to finish would probably be a poor use of time. We wanted users to be able to use the product for whatever training was suited to their needs. This policy decision met that goal.

TRANSFORMATIONAL RED TAPE

Managing change is never easy, and managing a major transformational change is even trickier. In higher education, tradition is very important, and that makes it hard to try something new. We began by forming partnerships with key decision makers, stakeholders, and a trusted vendor. Second, we started the project as a pilot with 50 users. A pilot is not threatening; it can also provide valuable feedback and evaluation to help make the real roll-out a success. And pilots can be ended without embarrassment. Next we made a plan and worked to that plan. Now that we had vendor partners for training, our role as IT professionals was to market the opportunity and provide guidance. Last but not least, we evaluated our project by meeting with focus groups and carefully examining use data.

Funding remains a challenge. In the first year, our CFO was able to find end-of-year funding. The second year we were able to move part of the funding into our regular budget and to receive grant funding. In the end, we moved the full cost of the initiative into our regular budget. Making room for funding takes time, creative strategies, and a vendor who will negotiate a reasonable educational price.

Significant change has taken place for Wellesley over the past two years as we transformed our training. Our pilot is complete, the Web-based training product has been implemented, and our new support structure is in place, but it is not time to ride into the sunset. We are working with our partners in the Boston Consortium to renegotiate vendor pricing and to develop a common list of core technology competencies for our employees and students. We need to continue to evaluate the new training program with our local partners and to be sure that funding is in place for the future. There is still a lot of work to do, but one thing is sure. We will be doing that work together since the Lone Ranger doesn't work here any more.

APPENDIX: CRAFTING A NEW SUPPORT STRUCTURE

The most difficult part of transforming a training program is "making work go away" in order to make room for the new initiative. Because IT service is often driven by user demand, it is hard to make space for something new. When do we decide to do away with a version that we support? When do we stop offering a poorly attended class? How do we add new classes to teach without abandoning others? As we prepared to offer our new Web-based software training, we looked carefully at our overall training program. Although we could not change it all overnight, we wanted to create a path to make some of our older, less successful strategies disappear and make space for the new. We developed several new support strategies:

Strategy 1: Deskside Coaching for faculty and staff

We hoped that most of our constituents would give the new Web-based training a try. But clearly, not everyone would prefer to learn this way or be able to do so for all situations. Some things that users need to learn to do are so specific to Wellesley that no off-the-shelf product is going to provide that training. Faculty constantly want us to come to them directly rather than work through our help desk. At the same time, we need faculty and staff to make calls to our help desk first so that they can be triaged and their problem either resolved or referred to the correct support person. But what we were hoping to create with Deskside Coaching was an opportunity for individual onsite training. Deskside Coaching is not for an emergency. It is not for fixing a computer that is misbehaving. It is not for something you need to accomplish in an hour. We handle those types of things through our normal help desk system. Deskside Coaching is a training program. Faculty and staff can call the help desk and request one-hour coaching slots to be scheduled in either the morning or the afternoon. Cards are mailed to all employees advertising the program, and they are told that they can sign up for individualized training at their desks on the following topics:

- Exploring the library's research resources;
- Microsoft Word, Excel, and PowerPoint;
- FirstClass mail and conferencing;
- Browsing the World Wide Web;
- Finding what you need on the World Wide Web;
- Navigating the Macintosh and Windows environments;
- Backing up and managing files;
- Updating virus-protection software.

Because the staff signs up in advance and the help desk just chooses an available slot, there is no back and forth trying to work out calendars to find a date that works. The help-desker just locates an available slot. It is expected that any of our support staff should be able to do a lesson on any of the topics. However, since the help desk knows our specialties, if they see a slot for one of us that specializes in the area being requested, they try to assign it to the expert. Staff and faculty understand that we will do the deskside lesson and go as far as we can or really as far as the user can. If more time is needed after the one-hour lesson, then we can refer it on to an expert for a follow-up.

When we started this program, we worried about how to keep up with the demand. Staff asked questions like, "What if I don't know that much about Excel, and I have to do a lesson on that?" But most people do not live in the preventive mode, so the number of requests was easily accommodated. The program keeps us on our toes because we have to be able to offer basic lessons in all the software that we support. And the support staff finds that it is *delightful* to go and help someone who wanted to learn and was not in a crisis. It is a pleasure we rarely get.

The positive responses have been phenomenal. Here is one of many wonderful comments we have received:

> "Thanks to you and your staff for the new initiative, Deskside Coaching. I had the pleasure of spending one hour yesterday with one of your staff. In that hour, I feel that I learned much more than I would have had it been a classroom setting. First of all, my questions were specific to my needs; secondly, I did

not feel intimidated. Then again, it could have been my 'teacher.' She is perfect for her job!"

We have received many similar comments. The program was so successful that we added library searching this fall. Those requests are referred to our reference librarians, and in the spring we plan to add lessons on using audiovisual equipment in our technology-equipped classrooms. The media services staff will do a one-on-one lesson in the person's classroom.

The success of this program has helped us "make work go away." Because we have this training safety net in place, we are now less hesitant to cancel classes with low enrollment. Our new guideline is that if a course has fewer than five attending, the instructor can opt to cancel the course and offer to do Deskside Coaching with the users or ask them to call the help desk when they want to schedule a session. This has been well received and has really encouraged the teaching staff. They were very tired of teaching to such small audiences. Also, we feel much more comfortable eliminating classes with typically low enrollments because we know a person can get an individual lesson. After our first semester of using the online training program, we stopped offering any introductory-level courses for Word, Excel, or operating systems. Those are now handled with self-paced online lessons or Deskside Coaching. In the place of those poorly attended intro courses, we have been able to offer more multimedia courses, such as Dreamweaver, which are very well attended. This was a win for both staff and users.

Strategy 2: Computing first aid for students

Instructional technology is so important in many of our courses at Wellesley. As faculty begin to use more and more software, digitizing, and so forth, in courses, students must master lots of technology. Faculty generally do not teach these software applications in class; they expect students to just "pick it up" on their own. Although online training can be helpful for this, sometimes students need a one-on-one lesson. Tutoring for general computer literacy topics is not part of a traditional tutoring program.

If you just need to learn how to prevent a page number from printing on the first page of a paper or cannot get your footnotes to behave, where are you going to go for help? What if you just do not understand how to make charts for a lab report? Or you are having trouble with the drawing tools in Photoshop? There are student consultants working in our public labs, but they are there for everyone who needs help in the lab. They cannot usually spend more than a few minutes with any one user. To address this problem we created a Computing First Aid Consultant program. Computing First Aid is the Wellesley student's rescue resource for immediate answers to questions about e-mail, electronic conferences, Microsoft Office, Dreamweaver, Fireworks, using the Internet, and other general computing topics. A brigade of specially trained Computing First Aid consultants is available on a drop-in basis five evenings a week from 7 to 9 P.M. Students can come in person and sit with the consultant for help, or they can use the First Aid Chat and just ask questions online. It is a convenient just-in-time tutoring option for general computer literacy or information literacy questions.

Strategy 3: Computing questions conference and chat

In addition to our Computing First Aid chat for students, we also offer a threaded online discussion conference for all community members. It is a place that anyone can ask any computing question. We ask all of the user services, network, repair, instructional computing, and help desk staff, as well as all of our student consultants, to read this conference and answer questions. Because of the student help we can answer questions pretty much 24/7. Someone is always up working on a paper! Community members who love technology, including lots of faculty, help with answering questions and giving technology advice. It has been very popular with the Wellesley community. If the question is beyond the scope of an online conference, the support staff members reply with advice on where to go for help on the particular question. It has been a great success and a wonderful addition to our other support efforts.

Strategy 4: Study breaks for students

We have found that professors really appreciate it when we are willing to offer focused one-hour sessions for their students on software that they need to use in class. For example, in our Quantitative Reasoning course, students need to use Excel right away. Many students in the course have insufficient experience with computing. We consult with the instructor and then teach a "quick start" class, usually from 4:15 to 5:15 P.M. This is outside of the lecture time for the course. We use the input from the instructor to prepare the demo. The attendance is excellent because it is advertised to the class by the professor. Faculty pick the date and time it will be offered, and we even have a sign-in sheet that is returned to the professors so they can see who attended. This type of targeted course has been very helpful for students. We have also done these types of classes on writing long papers with Word, creating original graphics, digitizing video, and designing Web pages, as well as on many other topics.

Strategy 5: One-on-one new employee orientation

Getting new employees off to a good start and teaching them about campus resources is critically important. At the beginning of the year we have to handle this as a class because of the large numbers. But after that initial rush, we handle our employee orientations as specialized one-hour Deskside Coaching sessions. During the session we help the users log into their accounts, do a tour of the campus information resources, and ensure that they understand how to get started with their new networked computers. We also make sure that they can log into their new online training account and know how to use the self-paced instruction. We explain the Deskside Coaching program and how to use our help desk. It is an effective and personal start for a new employee.

Strategy 6: Staff workshops

Similar to faculty workshops, this spring we began to offer staff workshops. We work with department managers to identify staff they feel would benefit from a concentrated training event. The employees are invited to plan a project and to attend a sequence of half-day workshops of concentrated instruction on topics that will contribute to their jobs and to completing their departmental project. This is a great way to move motivated staff to the next level of technology expertise.

Acknowledgment: I wish to express my thanks to MacKenzie Stewart, Rebecca Atwood, Mary Adele Combe, and the entire Wellesley Information Services staff for their dedication and support in the past two years in transforming our training programs. A special thanks is in order for Marylee Mutch from the Wellesley class of 2003 for her support and assistance in editing this chapter.

Chapter 8

Turning Coal into Diamonds: Organizing Under Pressure

JAY FERN
Manager of Online Learning

and

VINCE SHEEHAN
Chief Information Officer and Associate Dean for Information Technology, Indiana University School of Medicine

Oncourse is the funnest thing we get to do.

While it has all the complexities of any system that must be operational 24/7, it brings to life the real reason that we do what we do, which is to support the mission of teaching and learning.

Yet, it has not always been so fun.

The Oncourse story begins as a project that faced enormous pressures. For us, it was a lesson in how to take a vision expressed through strategic planning and turn it into reality.

The lesson was this: How we organized around the project was as important as the product we created.

THE BEGINNING

Oncourse was born in the midst of the transformation of the

technology environment and practices of Indiana University. It was a new concept in a new environment where the old rules did not apply.

During this period, many changes were underway on the technology front. The university created the position of Vice President for Information Technology. Reporting to the university president, the vice president was charged with developing a strategic technology plan for the university. This would include merging separate information services (IS) organizations on the two core campuses and creating reporting relationships with the six regional campuses. The resulting organization, University Information Technology Services (UITS), would be responsible for the creation and implementation of a strategic technology plan.

Of the 68 action items identified in the plan, two were foundational to our e-learning initiative:

> ACTION 12: To support course tools development and initiatives in distributed education, UITS should evaluate Web-based and other network-based learning environments and offer faculty a comprehensive set of options to easily create, edit, revise, and maintain online course material.
>
> ACTION 18: UITS should ensure an available and reliable infrastructure of networks, servers, storage, and applications for the support of online courses and other new learning experiences. (Indiana University, 1998)

In any planning process, so much time and energy is invested in creating the plan that, once published, there is a tendency to declare, "We're glad that's over." The reality is, it is just beginning.

History

Oncourse is Indiana University's e-learning system. It allows faculty and students to create, integrate, use, and maintain Web-based teaching and learning resources. For students, Oncourse presents learning tools in a single, consistent Web interface. For faculty, Oncourse provides a framework for building teaching environments that can include multimedia content and a wide range of online tools.

In an article published in the EDUCAUSE journal *CAUSE/EFFECT*, Dr. Garland Elmore, Associate Vice President of Teaching and Learning Information Technologies, described Oncourse this way:

> In late 1997 a re-evaluation of commercial products was motivated by the need to design and develop a Web-based Chemistry 101 course. This course became the focus of a project team of faculty and staff that helped define goals for a distributed learning environment that was recommended as part of the university's comprehensive information technology strategic plan. The WebLab first identified technical and functional requirements for the course. The major considerations were ease of use, scalability, and the potential to leverage legacy systems. Other considerations included alignment with university messaging strategies and the need to simplify individual Website publishing procedures. None of the off-the-shelf products could meet these requirements. Chemistry C101 was developed, therefore, using Java with a database backend. This experience helped establish a set of system requirements and tools that resulted in the development of Oncourse.
>
> Oncourse was developed uniquely to fit the IU environment. It takes advantage of university legacy systems to populate student and course templates automatically from existing information sources. Oncourse provides a shell for other university and commercial applications through a common interface. By its design, Oncourse facilitates dynamic creation of a personal Web site or profile for faculty and students. (Elmore, 1999)

Once the strategic plan was set, it was determined that the work done by the WebLab could be leveraged to create a university-wide tool to support those action items. Our goal was to provide a single system that would be centrally managed to meet the needs of all constituents.

The stage was set. A university-wide information technology services organization was in place. The strategic plan was complete and had identified the need for enterprise online teaching and learning tools. A prototype for Oncourse had been commissioned.

The best decision

One of the key ingredients for turning strategies into accomplishments is the organizational structure. We quickly recognized that we had two different types of organizing to do. The first was organizing for decision making and the second was organizing for delivering services.

A Chinese proverb states, "The ruler is like the wind; the subjects, like reeds. As the wind blows, so bend the reeds." Leadership often comes by example, and the tone for the Oncourse project was established at the top.

Senior leadership set the tone for the way work was to be done to implement Oncourse, seeking opportunities to succeed by sharing responsibility across organizational divisions. The associate vice presidents leading two of our five IS divisions (*see* www.indiana.edu/~uits/) established lines of authority for Oncourse decision making. The newly created Manager of Online Learning for the Teaching and Learning Division and the recently hired Director of University Information Systems would be coproject leaders. The decision about what to do had been made. Oncourse would be rolled into production as Indiana University's e-learning environment. It was now time to decide how to do it.

Making the wrong decisions for the right reasons

The ability to transform the Oncourse prototype into a production system required cooperation from many units across the university. We established an Implementation Team that brought together all the disciplines needed to move the project forward. The team's goal was to organize staff and processes to turn

Oncourse into a workable system, with all attendant support structures in place.

As the Implementation Team began its work, several factors came into play that dominated our decision making. The university had delayed setting an e-learning direction until the strategic planning process was complete. The beta version of Oncourse had been offered to a select group of faculty in the spring semester of 1998. Faculty interest grew quickly and more than 300 course accounts were generated in the first three months. The pressure from faculty to get this tool in place was beginning to swell.

Once the decision to move forward with Oncourse was made, the division heads established an aggressive timetable. It was announced that Oncourse would be available for the Fall 1999 semester. In order to allow faculty the time to set up a course within the environment, the system had to be released into production by the end of May 1999. The first meeting of the Implementation Team was in February 1999, giving us a little more than three months to get the job done. Even though the original system had an excellent conceptual design, it had not been tested for scale; three months was not enough time for implementation. We asked if the production date could be moved to the following semester, but the date had already been announced to the faculty, and there would be no deviation.

The pressure mounts

We were faced with what would be the first of many difficult decisions. While the prototype developers designed an excellent "proof of concept" system, the code was not ready-for-prime-time. Like most research and development efforts, it had begun as an experimental project and was still patched together in pieces rather than in a seamless, fluid design. To add to the complexity, all of the application components (Web server, database, application code, and file storage) were housed on a single physical server. The system required constant monitoring and tweaking to stay live. While this was workable in a prototype setting with a small number of courses, the architecture made it impossible to roll the system out for large-scale use.

In addition, one of the two original developers took another position within the university and was no longer available to contribute to the project. The application had no design documentation indicating naming conventions and database structures. If the remaining developer were to leave, there would be no one available who knew how the system was written.

We took immediate steps to address staffing issues. We created a development manager position and began recruiting internally to fill the vacancy for the second developer. While we now had a full staff, two of the three people knew virtually nothing about the code in the original application. From a personnel standpoint, the project had a single point of failure.

Pressure, pressure, and more pressure

Server management also became an immediate issue. Before the decision was made to share responsibility across organizational units, the Teaching and Learning Information Technology (TLIT) Division purchased servers for the Oncourse rollout. That division was responsible for desktop management and was in the process of selecting a vendor for a university-wide bulk purchasing agreement. One of the vendors offered highly discounted pricing on servers for Oncourse as an incentive to select their desktop. At the time, the TLIT Division expected to manage the Oncourse environment completely within their division, and the combination of the desktop pricing with the discounted price for the servers made this a sound financial decision.

While that decision created an overall benefit for the university, it created issues for the Oncourse rollout. Once we tried to implement the production servers, we encountered several problems. The servers were new models, and the vendor's technicians had little experience with them. Our systems administrators were unfamiliar with this new brand. The vendor was trying to implement a new clustering architecture that no one had experience with.

As the Implementation Team held its first meeting, we faced these pressures:

- A production date had been mandated. We were not yet sure what it would take to move Oncourse into production but had only three months to get it done.
- This was new territory as we were creating a dynamic environment, and not the traditional transaction processing application.
- The Oncourse code was in prototype mode and not ready for production level deployment.
- Only one developer had any knowledge of the code.
- The servers were new to our technicians and to our vendor.
- The servers were configured with a clustering architecture with which we had no experience.
- The two people leading the project (the authors) were new to their positions.

Not exactly a textbook formula for success.

Check your ego and your turf at the door

One of the more difficult discussions in those early days dealt with decisions concerning roles: which unit would provide which support service. Many team members were already involved in helping faculty with the existing version, and some team members were using the tool in courses they were teaching. There was a long list of bugs to be fixed and new features to be added. The normal tension between the support staff and the development team emerged. The developers viewed the clients and support people as unrealistic dreamers who were too demanding. The clients and support people viewed the developers as intransigent and unresponsive to their needs.

After two meetings, we held a discussion that brought the group into focus. It was agreed that the immediate goal was to get Oncourse into production mode as effectively as possible. To do this, we had to trust that each member had the best interests of the project—and, ultimately, the university—at heart. By the end of that meeting, we coined the phrase, "Check your ego and your turf at the door." This quickly became the motto of the team.

Building on what we already knew

Following the lead of the early implementation plan, our strategy for technical and pedagogical support built on a model that would leverage existing resources. Indiana University has won several awards for technical support in both its Knowledge Base application and Support Center processes. The university has experienced trainers for faculty and students in our education program. Each campus has a teaching and learning center where faculty get one-to-one training. Instead of building a silo and recreating these services just for Oncourse, we planned to leverage the expertise of those units that understand very well the needs of the clients we serve.

The project plan budget provided money for support staff in several areas. As a team, we decided to harness these centers of expertise. For example, rather than creating an Oncourse help desk, we leveraged those centers of expertise by providing an FTE ("full-time equivalent" staff member) for each of the existing Support Centers on the two core campuses. Those FTEs were integrated into the current Support Center operations, without requiring that they be dedicated to Oncourse. This model created a synergistic relationship within the entire support team. It encouraged each unit to become familiar with the application and distributed the support throughout the entire organization in a business-as-usual fashion. The same model was utilized in the user education program as well as in other Web services areas.

Weekly meetings provided updates on progress to the entire team and allowed us to get new issues on the table. Between meetings, impromptu sessions were held to deal with daily issues. Sometimes decisions had to be made on the fly, and in those cases the project leaders would confer and make a decision. All decisions were then communicated at the next weekly meeting. We were not always crystal-clear on what we were doing, but we had established tactical lines of authority and a communications process that kept everyone on the team informed. With the deadline looming, everyone worked feverishly and survived on little sleep and much caffeine. We hit each milestone, marked it off the list, and moved on to the next.

As we came within three weeks of the original target date, the team recognized there was still too much to do and asked to push the date back a week. While no one wanted to miss our target, we realized that it would be better to be a week late than to put out a bad product. We informed the senior leadership of the one-week delay and adjusted the project plan. One of the guiding principles of the Implementation Team was honesty: being realistic with ourselves and truthful with the people we reported to. By keeping leaders informed of the progress on a regular basis, and by giving them advanced warning of the delay, we got little argument and great support.

The first semester

While we were concerned as the first day of production approached, we knew we had prepared as well as we could in a short period of time. The team had worked well together and met deadlines: the various support structures and processes were all in place. Faculty began preparing courses and worked through the summer to get items posted and workflows organized within Oncourse. We encountered several problems with the architecture but worked through each one. The first day of classes came.

It was a disaster.

The three key weaknesses of the project—short timeframe, lack of familiarity with the code, and new hardware models—converged to create a perfect storm of frustration for faculty, students, and our team. The system crashed on a regular basis, and some days it was down more than it was up.

Throughout that first semester, we operated strictly in emergency management mode. We scrambled to put out fires on a moment-by-moment basis. There were so many problems we all held our breath whenever the phone rang, hoping we would not hear the words, "Oncourse is down again."

Much of the organizational structure we had designed had to be modified to meet the latest emergency. In the first few days there was some finger pointing, and we often heard "But I thought we agreed to . . ." whenever we discussed the problem du jour. In the middle of the second week of the semester, we called the team together and temporarily changed the rules. We agreed that the support and communications models we had developed were excellent for an established, stable system. However, we had to recognize that we were in emergency mode, and problems had to be triaged a different way. Assignments that had been clear in our preparation meetings might not work in the midst of multiple emergencies.

To present a unified voice to the university community, all decisions were routed through the two project leaders. There were often competing opinions about how to fix a certain problem, and we could not afford to experiment on the fly. We would meet as a team and discuss all the options; if a consensus could not be reached, then the two project leaders would make the call. We established that all ideas from every team member were valid for discussion, and that disagreements must be professional and rational. The goal for all of us was to make Oncourse a useful tool for faculty and students. Check your ego and your turf at the door; we had a job to do.

Throughout the semester, we worked though the problems until Oncourse was fairly reliable. Although there were numerous problems, our organizational structure made us accessible and responsive. Faculty knew whom to contact, and we replied to every query and complaint. While faculty often did not like what we told them, they appreciated the honesty of our answers. We did not try to hide our problems or blame them on anyone else.

The fact that we were working through every problem and communicating status regularly went a long way to establishing credibility. The clients were willing to give us some leeway in that first semester. While we had struggled to keep Oncourse going, faculty knew that this was a best-of-breed tool and its use had grown dramatically. The message from faculty was clear. You are on the right track; now let's work out the kinks.

MOVING ON: REORGANIZING TO DELIVER

Having survived the first semester, we evaluated our processes and gathered together what we had learned. Several key issues emerged concerning our ability to effectively deliver online teaching and learning services.

Stability

We recognized that a system had no value if it was not available, regardless of its functionality. If users cannot get to it, it is not useful—no matter how powerful it is.

Going into our second semester, the primary focus became the creation of an environment that was reliable, stable, and available. Given that Oncourse was now a production system used by several thousand faculty and students, this architectural change had to be phased in. We did not have the luxury of "blowing things up" and starting over. In addition, we did not want to make any radical changes in the middle of a semester. This left us with limited windows of opportunity in which major changes could be tested and deployed.

We developed a plan to deconstruct the code so that different modules could be housed on separate pieces of hardware. This allowed us to spread the workload of the most critical modules so that heavy usage of one piece would not bring the entire system down. We needed to physically separate specific components to achieve three goals: increase accessibility and response time, create redundancy of the environment, and enable better security measures.

Our plan called for a two-year staged process in which the reconfiguration of the hardware, database, and application code would be completed during semester breaks and holidays. With support from our senior leadership, we secured new sources of funding and expanded the development staff to a total of five developers.

Whereas the original model housed all functions on a single server, the plan was to move to a scalable environment with multiple entry points and load-balancing technology.

Refining the support model: The ah-hah moment

This changing Web environment showed us that the "project" is never done. There is a continuous need for improvement, restructuring, and evolution. In addition to stabilizing our technical environment, we needed to move away from crisis management to a stable organizational environment for both decision making and service delivery.

Due to its unique nature, managing Oncourse began to confirm the critical need for new approaches to existing services. One critical element was accounts management, because we populate Oncourse with daily downloads of course and roster information from our mainframe-based Student Information System.

As part of the ongoing integration of all eight campuses into a shared technology infrastructure, a project to merge User IDs from all campuses was underway. Prior to this, Username assignments had been a campus issue. It was critical for the authentication process within Oncourse that unique User IDs be established at the university level.

Cooperation across multiple units was called for once again. While the need for improved account management had already been identified, Oncourse served as the driving force to move the process forward.

As the application continued to gain acceptance across the university, it became clear that managing the Oncourse initiative was creating a sharp rise in critical support issues that seemed to be falling into a black hole. We began to ask the question, "Where are the holes in the support model?"

Once we began pulling all the issues together, the ah-hah moment came.

Partly because of new processes the Oncourse enterprise required, as well as the existing processes it depended on, we had to focus more attention on elements outside our direct control. If the system was not available, it made little difference to faculty and students whether it was an accounts problem, a network problem, or a problem with their own Internet service provider. It was an Oncourse problem. And in this business, perception is reality.

What began as an excellent concept of leveraging existing resources also became our weakest link. Front-line support was in the business of identifying problems and routing them to the appropriate people for resolution. The Development Team needed to focus on stability, application development, and bug fixes. Our existing support model had the Support Center handing off all problems directly to the Development Team. Critical issues that held the success of the application were not being resolved.

With the increasing reliance on legacy systems data and the growing number of clients that began pressing the IS organization into areas of support it had never encountered, we needed a point person who could negotiate the complexities.

This person would articulate the processes to the front-line support organizations and filter issues that were being sent directly to the Development Team. This position would also coordinate activities to correct data inconsistencies and accounts issues. Once again, the senior leadership supported our need for reallocation of funds from other sources and the position of Senior Online Support Analyst was created.

As we begin our sixth semester, 95 percent of all Oncourse related problem calls are resolved by the Support Center (tier one) or by the senior online support analyst (tier two). Only the problems directly associated with the code or the architectural environment are sent to the Development Team.

Communication: The final frontier

One of the more difficult issues we face is finding the most effective way to communicate. Getting the message out to the numerous constituencies in a university comprised of more than 100,000 faculty and students across eight campuses is a constant challenge.

In the earliest days, several people would respond to clients whenever an issue arose. The messages were not always clear and consistent. We decided to establish a guiding principle to speak with "one voice."

This required us to establish a working group that could identify communications needs and assign tasks to different units. Established under the guidance of the UITS Communications and Planning Office, membership includes every aspect of the process from developers to knowledge base creators to teaching and learning center personnel. Anyone who communicates with our clients is involved in this group.

Its charge is to set effective communication strategies for all documentation, application help, client education materials, publicity, and internal communication strategies. This group serves as the "checks and balances" component of the application development process. Because many of the members offer front-line support, they are able to clearly articulate our clients' needs. More importantly, they develop communication strategies from the middle, serving as a liaison between the client community and the IS organization. As use of Oncourse has grown exponentially, this group has been critical to the ongoing success of the initiative.

MOVING ON: REORGANIZING TO DECIDE

As Oncourse has grown over its six semesters, the process of determining enhancements has gotten more complex. When the number of clients was small, recommendations for improvements were easy to identify. The early adopters were well engaged and changes would affect only a few hundred faculty. Today, with over 50,000 active users of the system, these decisions are not as easy.

Getting buy-in: Just-in-time development

Oncourse is *for* Indiana University and *by* Indiana University. It is not for sale. Although on the surface, that statement may seem smug, it is intended to articulate our e-learning strategy as a university. There is also great internal marketing power in that notion. Strategically, we want our clients directing the process without concern that decisions are made with marketability to other institutions in mind. We try to make decisions based on what is best for Indiana University.

It is particularly gratifying when a faculty member suggests a change and sees it incorporated into the next release. It builds a sense of ownership and institutional pride, as well as tangibly proving that we are listening. It builds a sense of community around issues of teaching and learning that go far beyond the reaches of application development. This system improvement process has proven to be one of the most important strategic aspects of deployment.

To accomplish this user-responsive change, clients are encouraged to make suggestions in an online "suggestion box" located in the application. These suggestions are catalogued and used in focus group sessions separated by specific functionality. Once a cycle of suggestions has been catalogued, a formal call for focus group participation is communicated to the client community. Faculty sign up and, through a series of facilitated steps, begin to prioritize each suggestion for consideration as an enhancement. Each focus group submits a list to the development team to determine the scope of effort to incorporate each change. The process helps clients articulate needs and flesh out the best possible iteration of an enhancement.

Other suggestions come from scheduled demonstrations of how faculty use Oncourse. On a monthly basis, brown bag lunches are hosted by the Center for Teaching and Learning at the IUPUI campus. An instructor who uses Oncourse demonstrates how it is used in that particular course. Faculty members in the audience ask questions and suggest ways in which it might be useful in their own courses.

The Teaching and Learning Technologies Laboratory at our Bloomington campus hosts large-group sessions once a quarter. Several instructors demonstrate their use of the tools and answer questions about the pros and cons of different modules.

Originally created as a marketing device in the earliest days of Oncourse, these sessions provide valuable input to the improvement process. Oncourse team members attend each of these sessions, furiously scribbling notes on the recommendations.

As with any system, many suggestions about what we can do with Oncourse come through the Support Centers as clients encounter problems. While we occasionally receive suggestions from students telling us "Here's what you can do with Oncourse . . .," most suggestions are very helpful.

Steering them home

The final phase of the enhancement process involves the Teaching and Learning Steering Committee. The committee provides a university-wide view of Oncourse from a faculty perspective, as well as overall guidance to online learning initiatives in general. The steering committee receives the list of enhancements from the Development Team with a maximum number of development hours available for the next development cycle. The list is reviewed and prioritized based on long-term needs. Once prioritized, the Development Team begins the coding, testing, and implementation of the changes. As well, the Steering Committee oversees the strategic direction for future Oncourse use.

CONCLUSION: IT'S THE PROCESS, NOT THE PRODUCT

As we enter our sixth semester in production, our usage numbers have grown steadily. From fewer than a thousand users, Oncourse is now used by over 50,000 people. Usage varies from simple to complex. Some faculty simply post a syllabus and course announcements, while others deliver courses completely online.

Many lessons have been learned over the last three years, but the most important may be that it's the process, not the product. The way in which you organize to make decisions and organize to deliver and support the service are the critical success factors. If a product is sound, this process should be applicable in any environment.

If we had to do it over again, we would have pushed harder to have the production rollout delayed an additional semester. By creating a more controlled pilot process, we could have worked out the bugs in the system and put our support and response processes to the test in a less stressful environment.

As an institution, we are proud of the fact that we built Oncourse in-house and that it has proven to be successful. Without the ability to be flexible and agile in the application design and development process, some of our success might not have been as marked. Ultimately, the organization we designed and the processes we deployed worked for us. We believe these strategies can continue to work for us, whether the tool is built in-house or purchased.

All projects face varying levels of pressure. The key for us was organizing to work through those pressures and to create both the decision-making and delivery processes that would provide the best prospect for success.

REFERENCES

Elmore, Garland. 1999. "An Online Teaching and Learning Environment at Indiana University." *CAUSE/EFFECT* 22, no. 3. [Online]. Available: *www.educause.edu/ir/library/html/cem993d.html*. [10 April 2002].x

Indiana University. 1998. *Architecture for the 21st Century: An Information Technology Strategic Plan for Indiana University*. Bloomington: Indiana University Press.

Part IV

Developing New Leadership

Chapter 9

Organizing for Leadership: How University Libraries Can Meet the Leadership Challenge in Higher Education

ROBERT RENAUD
Director of the Waidner-Spahr Library and Associate Dean of the College, Dickinson College, Carlisle, Pennsylvania

and

ANNE MURRAY
Deputy Librarian, Cambridge University Library, Cambridge, England

INTRODUCTION

This chapter discusses the nature of leadership and its importance in higher education. It describes success factors in the development of leadership in the context of academic libraries, including mentoring, compensation systems, performance expectations and measures, diversity, professional development, and the role of organizational structure. It ends with specific thoughts and proposals in the areas of institutional self-interest, coherent HR strategies, interinstitutional cooperation, and continuing opportunities for leadership.

THE LEADERSHIP CHALLENGE

University libraries face a host of challenges as they enter a new century (Butcher, 1999; Hoadley, 1999). The cost of materials, particularly journals, typically far exceeds the rate of inflation and the increases granted by central budgeting authorities. New and emerging digital media based on the Internet compete for finite acquisitions funding with older, paper-based formats. The growth of interdisciplinary research confounds budgeting based on familiar disciplinary categories and leads to ever increasing specialization in journal and book publishing. The new digital formats themselves present challenges in terms of delivery, presentation, and preservation. The role of librarians, established by centuries of settled practice, is being questioned as faculty struggle to integrate new digital technologies into teaching, learning, and scholarship and seek assistance from academic librarians in finding robust solutions. Finally, profound changes in the economic and political order, such as the European Community and the North American Free Trade Agreement, are reshaping the commercial environment of scholarly publishing, increasing labor mobility, and introducing new structures for the management of intellectual property rights.

The library literature speaks eloquently to these challenges. Indeed, few professions can be said to have spent as much time contemplating its present and future role as have academic librarians. However, there is one challenge facing the university library that has received little sustained attention: the shortage of librarians able to provide leadership to respond to these trends. (The literature provides several valuable exceptions: Crosby, 2000; Riggs, 1999; Law, 2001; Bowlby, 1999; Dusky, 2001.) The lack of attention to this factor stands in stark contrast to the general management publications where the topic of leadership is a mainstay of the journal literature. There are several possible explanations for this inattention. It has been noted that librarians experience some discomfort with issues of management and leadership in an academic context, associating these topics with commercialism and superficiality (Agada, 1984; Black, 1981; Moore, 1983). It has even been suggested that librarians in leadership positions often lack the maturity and self-awareness needed to rise to the challenges facing their organizations (Quinn, 1999). Another reason relates to data collection. Academic libraries collect statistics relating to circulation and reference activity, collection size and growth, staffing, and budget. However, they seldom capture data that would serve to measure the recruitment, retention, and development of library managers. It can easily be argued that such data would be difficult to gather and to interpret. Nevertheless, the lack of data and research in this area neglects a rich opportunity to discuss the role of leadership in the future of the university library.

The lack of attention devoted to the issue of leadership in the library literature prompts a series of questions. What does leadership mean in the context of the university library? Is there a leadership shortage in university libraries? What evidence points to this shortage? How can university libraries develop new generations of leadership? A discussion of these questions leads us to consider the changes that are reshaping the university library and how we will, in the new century, need to address them.

THE NATURE OF LEADERSHIP

Before discussing the importance of leadership in the context of the university library, it is important to define the nature of leadership and to distinguish between leading and managing. These two terms are often used interchangeably. It is not uncommon, for example, for a position advertisement to require excellent managerial and leadership skills. While understandable, this use of language can lead us to think that leadership and management are simply aspects of the same activity. The management literature and our own experience suggest that this is not the case. John P. Kotter speaks to this distinction when he writes that leaders set directions and that managers cope with complexity by establishing systems and structures that create order (1990). The leader sees, articulates, and advocates where the organization needs to go. The manager establishes the controls necessary for large numbers of individuals to pursue those directions. Most importantly, leaders produce change, whereas managers organize to achieve those changes. Kotter uses a simple military analogy to make this point:

> [A] peacetime army can usually survive with good administration and management up and down the hierarchy, coupled with good leadership concentrated at the very top. A wartime army, however, needs competent leadership at all levels. No one yet has figured out how to manage people effectively into battle; they must be *led*. (1990: 104)

In making this distinction, it is also important to understand that both leadership and management are essential to the success of an organization. Without leadership, an organization cannot change to achieve new goals. Without management, an organization cannot produce the systems, structures, and planning processes to reach those goals. Successful organizations balance these traits by identifying, cultivating, and rewarding good leaders and managers and by recognizing that not everyone can be a leader and not everyone can be a manager.

As Kotter suggests, the balance of leadership and management varies according to challenges faced by organizations. During periods of relative stability, the strengths of management predominate. Here, careful planning, budgeting, and hierarchical organizations ensure consistency and constancy. During periods of instability, the capacity of these mechanisms to cope with rapid change is overwhelmed, creating the need to augment management with leadership. The list of challenges facing university libraries cited above suggest that we live in a period of instability that requires an emphasis on leadership over management.

If the experience of other organizations provides any guidance, we can expect that university libraries are, to cite Kotter, "overmanaged and underled" (1990: 103). Both anecdotal and empirical evidence of this problem and the shortage of librarians able to lead into the future abounds. Searches for university librarians and senior managers often take months and even years. In some cases, searches are abandoned altogether while university libraries try to reorganize to manage around the vacancy. Whereas senior university librarians served long tenures in the past, it is now not unusual for a recently recruited manager to move on to a new opportunity in a matter of months or a few years. The addition of information technology to the portfolio of some university librarians adds to this volatility as institutions attempt to recruit from a small pool of talented individuals expert in both librarianship and technology (Renaud, 2001). As we enter the new century, demographic changes, at least in the United States, compound the problem, as library directors from the "baby boom" generation retire, creating an anticipated increase in vacancies between 2010 and 2020 (Munde, 2000).

Further evidence of this leadership challenge exists in the form of institutional responses such as the Frye Leadership Institute. This institute, supported by a grant from the Robert W. Woodruff Foundation and sponsored by the Council on Library and Information Resources, EDUCAUSE, and Emory University, brings together 40 to 50 librarians, information technology managers, and teaching faculty for an intensive two week program of lectures, seminars, and presentations (Marcum and Hawkins, 2000). By identifying and cultivating potential leaders, the Frye Institute consciously addresses the leadership challenge facing university libraries, computing centers, and academic departments.

SUCCESS FACTORS

If university libraries need leadership to thrive in the new century, we need to identify those factors that must be present in order for future leaders to be developed. In describing these factors, we need to move beyond the assumption that "leaders are born, not made." The experience of private sector organizations clearly contradicts this assumption. The Royal Dutch/Shell Group in the United Kingdom and General Electric in the United States, for example, have set a high value on the identification and development of future managers and have created within their organizations programs on the scale of the Frye Leadership Institute to achieve this goal (Fulmer, Gibbs, and Goldsmith, 2000). These companies do not pursue these programs simply because they believe that education is inherently a good thing. They create these programs as a strategic effort to achieve competitive advantage. University libraries need to identify and implement programs that will enable them to achieve similar benefits.

MENTORING

Most successful people can point to the value of key mentoring relationships over the course of their careers. Despite this, the "mentor/protégé relationship, although recognized for centuries, remains an elusive phenomenon" (Munde, 2000: 172). For some, mentoring carries a negative connotation, as in the phrase "old boys" network, in that it tends to reinforce existing elites. At an extreme, Janice J. Kirkland writes of "antimentoring" or the intentional withholding of advice and support from certain groups such as women (1997: 383). Here mentoring, or its absence, perpetuates an elite based on gender. For most observers, mentoring suggests both formal and informal relationships that can help to identify and cultivate leaders. The power of these relationships to shape careers and career choices over time is undisputed. Exactly how to implement such relationships in university libraries is more problematic. Most mentoring relationships appear to occur accidentally, as mentor and the mentored meet by chance or on the basis of a shared interest or trait. Some leaders, including some university librarians, see mentoring as an essential part of their roles and actively seek to find and assist younger professionals. Although valuable, mentoring relationships based on chance encounters or the interests of senior managers leave much to be desired. As noted above, mentors sometimes seek out librarians in their own image, thereby unconsciously not selecting librarians of other genders, backgrounds, or races. For minority professionals in particular, this natural tendency can work to limit career mobility and can inhibit the organization's ability to identify new talent (Thomas, 2001; Enomoto, Gardiner, and Grogan, 2000). A more promising, if also imperfect, approach consists in formal mentoring programs instituted by the university library in a conscious attempt to develop new leaders. At the University of

Delaware, for example, a multilevel mentoring program moves library staff from simple orientation to in-depth career mentoring. However, such efforts appear to be the exception rather than the rule. In practice, most existing programs "do nothing to prepare employees for career advancement to higher positions interim or otherwise, or for redeployment to other functional positions" (Munde, 2000: 173).

PERFORMANCE EXPECTATIONS AND MEASURES

The relative lack of attention paid to leadership in academic librarianship relates at least in part to the absence of formal performance measures in higher education comparable to those in private firms. The management literature points again and again to the imperatives of competitive advantage, measurable in financial terms, as a justification for a corporate focus on identifying and developing leaders. Particularly during periods of volatile change, the ability of a corporation to produce leaders is seen as crucial and the investments made in promising staff as essential. At General Electric, for example, the company's belief in the role played by leadership means that the corporate executive development center is the only unbudgeted and unmeasured unit in the company (Fulmer, Gibbs, and Goldsmith, 2000: 50). For the university library, a justification based on measurable outcomes does not exist. Although libraries measure many activities, and attempts at estimating returns on investment have been made, the types of clear performance measures that help to illuminate effective individuals within the university library are few and far between. In particular, for more junior librarians who may not come to the attention of the library director, opportunities to develop and display leadership ability are rare. This creates a dilemma for all involved. For the university librarian, judgments about individual librarians become subjective and draw on the perceptions of supervisors and peers. For more junior librarians, efforts to develop leadership skills and to become visible to senior managers can be frustrated. Here, the challenge is to find ways for ambitious librarians to grow into leaders in an environment where little is measured that can distinguish individual promise.

COMPENSATION AND REWARDS

The absence of performance measures contributes in part to another impediment to the development of leadership in university libraries: compensation and reward systems. Most university libraries in Europe and the United States compensate librarians as they progress through a salary structure based on rank and seniority. In institutions in which librarians have faculty status, this system rewards librarians who publish, assume leadership in professional organizations, and receive recognition in various forms from their peers. This orderly pattern of career progression reflects the values of management, not of leadership. It rewards outward professional efforts while ignoring the development of the individual librarian as an agent of change within the home organization, that is to say, as a leader. It also tends over time to a conservatism based on established forms of recognition and status. This poses a problem for the university library as a whole. The library may unintentionally, through its compensation system, reinforce patterns of resistance to change and also frustrate potential leaders. Here, compensation and rewards communicate values to the university library staff, values that may undermine the long-term effectiveness of the organization. For junior librarians, this structure presents a limited set of alternatives. The librarian may choose to stay and wait for a leadership opportunity. The more ambitious librarian is more likely to move to another university library where a fresh start in a new position will provide new challenges and opportunities to come to the attention of senior librarians. While a degree of personnel turnover is healthy, losing future leaders for this reason also entails wasted potential and opportunity.

PROFESSIONAL DEVELOPMENT

The experience of private sector firms indicates that the development of future leaders requires significant investments in professional development and education. As noted above, many large European and American companies operate their own management development centers and allow their executives to attend them for prolonged periods. For most university libraries, this is not the case. Although central personnel offices may arrange for supervisory and management training offered by university staff or by outside agencies, the type of sustained and serious leadership development institutes found in the private sector are rare. The decentralized nature of higher education leaves this responsibility to professional organizations such as the SCONUL (Society for College, National and University Libraries) or CURL (Consortium of University Research Libraries) in the United Kingdom, the Association of Research Libraries in the United States, and independent, grant-funded organizations such as the Frye Leadership Institute. While valuable, these programs vary widely in their approaches and have a limited capacity to accommodate large numbers of librarians. The absence of sustained opportunities for most librarians to hone leadership skills leaves professional development, like mentoring, to chance. It also suggests to librarians that leaders are "born, not made," and that efforts to develop leadership skills are not justified.

DIVERSITY

The library literature has in recent years recognized the value of diversity from several perspectives. From the ethical perspective, concerns about diversity speak to the nature of librarianship as a profession within society. Like freedom of speech, opposition to censorship, and open public access, diversity is a value that librarians bring to civic life. This has been expressed more generally by landmark legislation such as the Sex Discrimination Act of 1970 and Equal Pay Act of 1975 in the United Kingdom and the Civil Rights Act of 1964 in the United States. In addition to the ethical arguments, diversity also speaks to the leadership challenge. If we assume that leaders can appear at any level of the organization, we need to ensure that all individuals experience opportunities to develop and exhibit leadership potential. As Irene Owens writes, this imperative goes far beyond "diversity training" and instead addresses the need for senior university librarians to take diversity issues seriously and model openness to the contributions of all staff (2000: 20). This is a pragmatic, in addition to an ethical, consideration. In the United States, for example, approximately 85 percent of those entering the workforce are female, African American, Asian American, Latino, or new immigrants (Owens, 2000; Nardoni, 1997). A proactive approach to diversity helps to ensure a continuous stream of new talent.

ORGANIZATIONAL STRUCTURE

University libraries vary widely in their organizational structure. However, two broad categories have emerged in recent years: hierarchical, command-driven and flat, team-driven. In hierarchical structures, a pyramid exists in which authority flows from the university librarian down a clear chain of reporting relationships. In order to manage large numbers of librarians and staff, the library is divided up into units typically headed up by librarians. These units receive direction from layers of managers and supervisors communicating information from the university librarian and possibly a small leadership group. This structure clarifies responsibilities, communicates the instructions of its leadership, and serves to control and stabilize the organization. Here, the flow of information within the organization is one way: top-down. In contrast, the flat organizational structure removes layers of managers and supervisors and tends to use team-based approaches. The university librarian in a flat organization acts more as a facilitator than as a traditional manager, seeking to develop the ability of the library to respond to change through consensus and group problem solving. Here, the flow of information is two way: up-down and down-up. Needless to say, these simple characterizations do not exactly fit most libraries. Many university libraries use a wide range of organizational structures that combine elements of the hierarchical and the flat models.

These categories overgeneralize the differences between university libraries. Nevertheless, they provide a basis for discussing how libraries are organized and how this affects leadership development. In hierarchical structures, leadership is concentrated at the top whereas management—that is to say, the implementation of the university librarian's vision—takes place at lower levels. Here, opportunities for leadership grow out of the ability of the individual librarian to display conspicuous talent at implementing the direction set by senior management. In flat organizations, leadership opportunities occur at all levels of the organization since authority is dispersed and layers of management and supervision have been reduced. Although no empirical evidence exists to support this assertion, it might be expected that university libraries with flat organizations might be more successful than those with hierarchical structures in producing future leaders, since they expose a broader range of librarians and staff to managerial challenges. Despite this, it is also most likely the case that leaders in academic librarianship emerge from every type of organizational structure and from a wide variety of career paths.

PROPOSALS

The challenges facing university libraries clearly call out for leadership. However, as has been demonstrated, significant obstacles to the development of future leaders exist. Haphazard attempts at mentoring can leave promising librarians to fend for themselves. Compensation and reward systems based on seniority rather than performance communicate the values of management over leadership. Institutions of higher education, operating in relative isolation, cannot provide the sustained leadership training often found in the private sector. As the workforce becomes more diverse, it is essential that senior managers recruit from across the community. Organizational structures based on hierarchies can stifle individual acts of leadership and obscure the presence of librarians of high potential.

Despite these obstacles, the university library has enormous opportunities to identify, develop, and promote future leaders. The following proposals address the leadership challenge in university libraries.

RECOGNIZE THE NEED FOR LEADERSHIP

For librarians familiar with the stability and predictability of the university library in earlier decades, the need to lead, as well as manage, may not be clear. Senior library managers therefore need to describe the new context in which university libraries find themselves and the limits of conventional management processes to respond effectively to it. In the collegial culture of the university library, making the case for the development of promising individuals requires some imagination. It also requires a broad understanding of the need to develop leaders who will benefit higher education as a whole and not just individual institutions. As labor mobility increases with the advent of economic structures such as the European Community and the North American Free Trade Agreement, institutions may experience a natural reluctance to invest in librarians only to have them leave for new opportunities. Here, the need exists to understand that a certain degree of managerial turnover is normal and healthy and that institutions must challenge promising librarians who demonstrate leadership potential. A broad perspective on the need for leadership in higher education as a whole enables everyone to understand the relationship between such short-term investments and the long-term health of academic librarianship.

CREATE COHERENT INSTITUTIONAL STRATEGIES

After the need for leadership is established, senior management needs to establish coherent strategies for identifying, developing, and training librarians with leadership potential. For university libraries, this includes working with the central human resources department to include leadership as a criterion in personnel evaluations and training programs. Librarians under evaluation need to understand what leadership, in contrast to management, is and to perceive the benefits of developing themselves as leaders. Since leadership entails the acceptance of risk, rather than its avoidance, senior management must emphasize the value of risk taking and find opportunities to celebrate "constructive failures" that advance the library as a whole. Apart from public recognition, compensation and reward structures must be adjusted to reinforce these values. Particularly for publicly funded universities, this presents real challenges. Nevertheless, there is no substitute for the role of compensation and advancement in communicating the need for leadership in the new century. Finally, the university library needs to engage in formal succession planning that identifies the competencies needed to rise to leadership positions and the individuals under consideration for these opportunities (Schall, 1997; Bridgland, 1999).

SUPPORT AND CREATE LEADERSHIP DEVELOPMENT INSTITUTES

The experience of the private sector clearly demonstrates the value of sustained, formal, and substantive leadership development training. This training creates spaces for promising individuals to study leadership, meet with successful leaders, and consider the career choices that face them. It also signals to the organization the value and necessity of leadership. Unlike large multinational corporations, university libraries seldom possess the resources to mount such institutes. They therefore need to support efforts such as the Association of College and Research Libraries, Harvard Leadership Institute and the Frye Institute and to advocate new programs. The cost to university libraries, in terms of direct costs and absence of key staff, entails real sacrifices. However, if these investments are not made, opportunities to develop new generations of leadership will be lost.

MOVE FROM OPERATIONAL TO PROJECT-BASED WORK

In private sector firms, leaders become visible because performance measures are relatively clear. The measures of profit and loss, market share, customer satisfaction, and product innovation highlight high performers and future leaders. In the university library, few such measures exist. As noted above, this leaves the identification of future leaders to the judgment of managers and supervisors and therefore to the vagaries of individual subjective impressions. It is in practice very difficult to identify leadership potential in the context of day-to-day, operational work. In contrast, project-based work serves to highlight individual contributions, innovation, and leadership potential. If properly framed, a project has objectives, measures of success, deliverables, and a specific beginning and end. This allows the individual librarian assigned to a project to "own" it in a way impossible in the context of operational activities and to demonstrate both leadership potential and managerial ability. It also allows the university librarian to "audition" promising librarians who may in the future become line managers responsible for operational departments. In fact, the advantages of project-based work in helping to develop librarians and to hone the capacities of the university library are such that it may be valuable to seek opportunities to convert operational work to projects in general.

THINK OUTSIDE OF THE PROFESSIONAL BOX

Identifying and developing a new generation of leadership in academic libraries will require imagination and the willingness to innovate. While librarianship contains a core of values and practices essential to success, it is also necessary to think "outside the box" and consider options that expand the alternative sources of future talent. For example, up to this point it has been assumed that future leaders in university libraries will primarily be professional librarians. This may be the case. However, support staff within the library, or staff from other parts of the university, may also present leadership potential. University libraries increasingly turn to the private sector for new ideas and an opportunity to change institutional cultures. The individuals recruited in this way may or may not have the credentials normally expected of academic librarians. It may be useful to consider either hiring managers who do not possess such credentials or who are willing to obtain them later. By looking beyond the conventional pool of professional talent, the university library may benefit from fresh perspectives, innovative practices, and new leadership.

INSTITUTIONALIZE LEADERSHIP IN PROFESSIONAL EDUCATION

If leadership is essential to the future of the university library, it needs to institutionalize in a way that communicates its importance to those entering and working in the profession. In other words, the role of leadership needs to be embedded into the professional education that librarians receive and must become a criterion in the selection of candidates for these programs. This runs against the grain of library education as it now exists, with its emphasis on technical competencies and purely operational issues. At present, the curricula of professional library programs send a muted message. Even though leadership is sometimes mentioned as an important factor in admissions decisions, actual course offerings seldom address its importance or role. In contrast, professional management programs often place a high priority on leadership and recognize its value in terms of long-term competitive advantage. The mission statement of the Harvard Business School's MBA program, for example, places a primary emphasis on leadership, almost to the exclusion of all else:

> The mission of the MBA Program at Harvard Business School is to develop outstanding business leaders who will contribute to the well being of society. It is this mission that guides the HBS experience and inspires graduates to go out there and make a difference. (Harvard University, n.d.)

A fresh emphasis on leadership in library education would help to clarify the future role of librarians in higher education and would greatly assist in the selection of new professional librarians. It would encourage library schools to explore underserved populations such as women and minorities for overlooked individuals. It would suggest that persons who have excelled in other careers might move into leadership roles in university libraries and that the curricula of professional library schools should be modified to accommodate career changers. It is possible that not all library schools would want to, or be able to, make this transition. Indeed, not all MBA programs place a strong emphasis on leadership potential. However, even a small number of library schools that emphasize leadership over technical skills would help towards alleviating the shortage of candidates for the next generation of senior positions.

CONCLUSION

The university library faces a host of challenges that require the vision, energy, and direction of leadership. However, the culture of academic librarianship, with its emphasis on technical tasks, day-to-day work, and stable managerial practices, inhibits the development of leaders. The profession needs to recognize the value of leadership and encourage its development through training, compensation, and advancement. An increasingly diverse workforce deepens the talent pool to be explored and recruiting outside normal professional channels promises to bring new insights and innovation. The profession needs to take risks, to hire on potential rather than only considering candidates with library qualifications. Within each institution opportunities must be provided for librarians to "lead from the middle." To thrive in this era of rapid change, academic institutions have to be led by librarians who are genuinely excited by and committed to change. In the short term, those who currently hold leadership positions have a duty to the profession to ensure that potential leaders of the future are groomed for positions where they will need a variety of generic, technical, and specialist skills. Equally, librarians themselves will have to take advantage of any opportunity to gain experience outside their current roles. In the long term, the curriculum at library schools must take into account the diverse range of skills needed to progress in a library career and include both management and leadership skills in the curriculum. In summary, it will involve a sectorwide strategy. If academic librarians fail to take action, the pool of suitable candidates for university librarian positions will become smaller and the skills gap larger. If they rise to the leadership challenge, academic librarians will continue to play a vital role in the success of higher education.

REFERENCES

Agada, John. 1984. "Studies of the Personality of Librarians." *Drexel Library Quarterly* 20, no. 2 (Spring): 24–45.

Black, Sandra M. 1981. "Personality—Librarians as Communicators." *Canadian Library Journal* 38, no. 2 (April): 65–71.

Bowlby, Raynna. 1999. "Learning to Lead." *College and Research Libraries News* 60(April): 292–293, 318.

Bridgland, Angela. 1999. "To Fill, or How to Fill: That is the Question. Succession Planning and Leadership Development in Academic Libraries." *Australian Academic and Research Libraries* 30 (March): 20–29.

Butcher, Karyle. 1999. "Reflections on Academic Librarianship." *The Journal of Academic Librarianship* 25 (September): 350–353.

Crosby, John. 2000. "Water, Water Everywhere, But Not a Drop to Drink." *Information Outlook* 4 (October): 17.

Dusky, Kathy L. 2001. "Library Leadership in Times of Change." *PNLA Quarterly* 65 (Winter): 16–20.

Enomoto, Ernestine K., Mary E. Gardiner, and Margaret Grogan. 2000. "Notes to Athene: Mentoring Relationships for Women of Color." *Urban Education* 35: 567–583.

Fulmer, Robert M., Philip A. Gibbs, and Marshall Goldsmith. 2000. "Developing Leaders: How Winning Companies Keep on Winning." *Sloan Management Review* 42 (Fall): 49–61.

Harvard University. Harvard Business School. [M.B.A. mission statement]. [Online]. Available: *www.hbs.edu/mba/experience/index.html*. [8 April 2002].

Hoadley, Irene Braden. 1999. "Reflections: Management Morphology—How We Got to Be Who We Are." *Journal of Academic Librarianship* 25 (July): 267–273.

Kirkland, Janice J. 1997. "The Missing Women Library Directors: Deprivation versus Mentoring." *College and Research Libraries* 58 (July): 376–384.

Kotter, J. P. 1990. "What Leaders Really Do." *Harvard Business Review* 68 (May/June): 103–104.

Law, Margaret. 2001. "Nothing Ventured, Nothing Gained." *PNLA Quarterly* 65 (Summer): 7–9.

Marcum, Deanna B. and Brian L. Hawkins. 2000. "The Frye Leadership Institute: A Unique Opportunity for a Unique Problem." *EDUCAUSE Review* 35 (November/December): 8–9.

Moore, May M. 1983. "'New Blood' and Managerial Potential in Academic Libraries." *Journal of Academic Librarianship* 9 (July): 142–147.

Munde, Gail. 2000. "Beyond Mentoring: Toward the Rejuvenation of Academic Libraries." *Journal of Academic Librarianship* 26(May 2000): 171–175.

Nardoni, Ren. 1997. "Competency-Based Succession Planning." *Information Systems Management* 14 (Fall): 60–62.

Owens, Irene. 2000. "A Managerial/Leadership Approach to Maintaining Diversity in Libraries." *Texas Library Journal* 76 (Spring): 20.

Quinn, Brian. 1999. "Librarians' and psychologists' view of leadership: Converging and diverging perspectives." *Library Administration and Management* 13 (Summer): 149.

Renaud, Robert. 2001. "What Happened to the Library? When the Library and the Computer Center Merge." *College and Research Libraries News* 60 (November): 987–989.

Riggs, Donald. 1999. "Academic Library Leadership: Observations and Questions." *College and Research Libraries* 60 (January): 6–8.

Schall, Ellen. 1997. "Public-Sector Succession: A Strategic Approach to Sustaining Innovation." *Public Administration Review* 57 (January/ February): 4–11.

Thomas, David A. 2001. "The Truth About Mentoring Minorities: Race Matters." *Harvard Business Review* 79: 98–108.

Chapter 10

Rising to the Top: The Peculiar Leadership Challenges for the Successful Internal Candidate

Elizabeth D. Hammond
Dean of University Libraries, Mercer University

THE INSTITUTIONAL VIEW

The search for a new library leader can be an exciting and unsettling experience for the library organization. A number of individuals will be involved in shaping the search, which inevitably brings more scrutiny to the library, its employees, and its operations. What are the strengths and weaknesses of the organization? What are we looking for in a new leader? What skills and abilities are needed at this point in the life of the library and the institution? How does the institution recruit and evaluate candidates? Library employees and university administration may have different opinions about the state of the library or the degree to which improvements and changes are needed. Working through those issues should lead to an agreement on the qualities desired in a new library administrator and possibly to a unified, shared vision for the future of the library.

Those conducting the search are faced with many decisions in shaping the process. Often, the search committee will find there are internal candidates for the position. This adds a particular dynamic to the search process that can create special challenges for the search committee, the institution, and the candidate. This chapter is a study of that particular situation and the leadership challenges for the successful internal candidate.

First, what is leadership? Leadership is bringing together different abilities and ideas into a coherent path for the institution. Leadership is about trust, vision, and commitment. The leader must be committed to the unit and its vision, and he or she must trust those who will contribute to reaching that vision. The staff in turn must trust the leader and commit to the goals and ideals of the unit's work in order to reach a common vision. A leader cannot lead without followers; followers look to a leader to represent them and their needs effectively. Simply put, a leadership role is conferred by the followers. Any successful candidate must be able to project and exemplify those key leadership qualities. The wise internal candidate will carefully assess the situation and be mindful of the dynamics affecting his or her candidacy. Effectiveness as the future leader begins when you apply for the job and carries through how you handle yourself through the search process, how you establish or change working relationships, how you relate to your colleagues, and, most of all, how you project a vision for the organization and institution.

THE INTERNAL CANDIDATE'S PERSPECTIVE

Becoming a candidate from within is very different from applying from outside and can be a real advantage. Several librarians who have been through the process as internal candidates report (in personal communications) that knowing the organization, the people, the culture, and the problems can provide a tremendous headstart when applying for the leadership position. Jean Dowdall (2000) wrote that "there may be problems at your institution but at least you know what they are . . . you know what the job is about from observing the person leaving the position, so you can get a quicker start than if you had changed institutions." As an insider, you are likely to be better known than an external applicant, which has advantages and disadvantages. You may already be viewed as an "heir apparent," depending on the current position, a successful career path, or the nature of work assignments that have exposed you to a wide range of colleagues who view you as a successful leader. In some situations, the internal candidate may have enough support among colleagues to be sought out and encouraged to apply by library colleagues or friends within the organization. Conversely, the potential internal candidate may be viewed as an ambitious, self-serving individual who desires to become "the boss" over current colleagues. Your own ambition, as evidenced by your candidacy, can be alienating to those who feel challenged or threatened by a potential change in the pecking order and direction of the library.

What is the internal candidate up against? Some involved in the search process may feel strongly that an outsider is best for the current situation, someone with new, fresh ideas to contribute beyond what current employees are thought to offer. There is a tendency to invest an external candidate from outside the immediate area with an almost omniscient quality; a candidate coming from another institution may appear more experienced or more effective than someone already in the organization. People in the organization may also view the outsider as the solution to all their problems. This so-called "50 mile rule" can pose a challenge to the internal candidate. (The definition of an expert is someone "from 50 miles away.") It is critical that you effectively articulate ideas, insights, and a vision that come from a comprehensive knowledge of libraries and higher education. This may be particularly challenging for long-term employees who, on paper, may seem to show limited experience at other institutions but have in fact established a powerful network of colleagues and contacts around the country. Professional involvement can be documented on a *vita;* demonstration of a broad sense of knowledge and practices must come across in other application documents, work references, and the interview conversations. The internal candidate must transcend the stamp of familiarity and the status quo and truly be seen as an independent free thinker who uses the capacity to think outside the box while capitalizing on knowledge of the current institution. People who think they already know the internal candidate might need to learn for the first time that she can work effectively to bring about change and improvements based on broad knowledge.

The internal candidate may be scrutinized more closely because people know enough about her to quickly sense which areas of questioning or investigation to pursue. She must present her accomplishments in a new light: what she has done, what she has said, the things she has written, the alliances she has forged, and the challenges she has faced and overcome. She cannot and should not suddenly become something she is not—a new persona as a candidate—if she wants to be taken seriously. Since she has a record and reputation, she has to use that to full advantage.

It may be a challenge for the internal candidate to present herself as an independent person and potential leader for the organization if she worked closely with the former director. If there have been problems in the organization, she may be considered to have contributed to them. People want to know how she fitted into the past administration. She needs to balance loyalty to the former leader with integrity about her own perspective. Was she a loyal employee whose profile and value in the organization came primarily from dutifully supporting the administration? Did this role work well for her or cause friction between her and her colleagues? Or while loyal, did she seek new ideas for the organization and build working relationships across the institution? If the organization is considered to be strong, all of this may be easier. According to Dowdall, "If there has been great institutional success and the insider is perceived to have been part of that success, there may be some preference for the insider." In any case, the successful internal candidate must present independent thinking and plans for the institution. In short, the aspiring candidate must be viewed as his or her own person, sufficiently creating a distance from the prior administration in order to set forth an independent vision for the unit and the institution.

INTERIM LEADERSHIP: CHALLENGES AND OPPORTUNITIES

The internal candidate knows the organization well and can speak to the issues of the position and institution with knowledge and preparation. Appointment as the interim leader may offer the chance to "act the part" for some period of time. People within the organization can get a sense of how the internal candidate communicates, how she makes decisions, what her priorities are, and how she relates to the rest of the institution. While an internal interim leader may not have the freedom, or the desire, to make significant changes in an acting capacity, this is an opportunity to demonstrate talents in a new light. Before accepting such a position, a potential internal candidate must consider the possibility that interim leadership can sometimes be a disadvantage. If there are difficulties in the organization, the search committee may tend to look at the interim leader as part of the problem, rather than as a real chance for new and successful leadership. An interim leader must always position himself or herself to gracefully return to work with colleagues in the former working relationships. She must provide effective leadership without burning bridges with current colleagues.

Working relationships with colleagues inevitably change when one staff member officially becomes a candidate for leadership. Certain kinds of casual conversations with colleagues become inappropriate; for example, conversations about personnel or discussions of unpopular library decisions. The internal candidate fills a different role in discussions, and colleagues may become a bit aloof. The candidate's behavior must be above reproach. Even those who support her candidacy may be uncomfortable with what they perceive as "too much" ambition. They also realize that if she is selected, she may appreciate their strengths but will know too much about their weaknesses. Everyone is waiting to see what the final hiring decision will be. All the participants view each other in a new light—what does the internal candidate think about old friends and colleagues now? What changes might she like to make? Who are her allies? Where are the problems and challenges? She is seeking a chance to provide leadership; what is she hoping to do?

THE ORGANIZATIONAL VIEW

The choice between an insider or outsider can be complicated. Some organizations see the insider as a safe choice, someone invested in the organization and therefore likely to continue the established path. Looking outside is more of a gamble. In the search process, Stephanie Overman (1994) recognizes that "candidates naturally try to show themselves in the best light . . . hiding weaknesses. With an inside candidate you know what they are. But for the outsider, you don't know what they are and so can't plan for them."

In many respects, an internal appointment can be good for the individual and good for the organization. It says something positive about personnel management and the culture when the institution supports its own and provides opportunities for advancement and recognition. Gary Kaplan (1999) reminds us that "a healthy organization first looks to its in-house talent pool for possible promotion, as both a morale booster and cost-saving approach. Employees view each outside hire as an in-house failure to develop their own skills and opportunity within the organization. Visible vertical process helps retention by signaling a future for current employees. Unless talented people feel there are opportunities within the company to deepen and expand their managerial skill through increasing responsibilities, they are likely to seek the same elsewhere." The successful internal candidate should nurture and foster that supportive organizational culture by encouraging others to develop their own skills for professional development and advancement while working with the leadership on a shared vision for the organization.

On the other hand, an organization in distress may need an outsider to solve significant problems or bring fresh perspectives, or as Julie Cohen Mason (1992) puts it, "to step into the fray to shake up a staid company, purge a company ridden with scandal, or take command of a company that had no succession plan." In these extreme situations, it may be impossible for an internal candidate to succeed if the larger organization is looking for significant change. This can be paradoxical; the internal candidate may understand the organization's problems better than any other candidate can.

The candidate can seize the chance to clearly identify the things that are needed for the organization to grow and improve, for example, funding, personnel, space, or different reporting lines within the institution. On the other hand, it is often more difficult to negotiate for necessary resources as an internal candidate. In fact, pushing the point too firmly may alienate the administration. The internal candidate must find a way to effectively alert the administration to organizational needs and expectations. In the long run, this will prove beneficial and set the tone for the future.

THE SUCCESSFUL INTERNAL CANDIDATE

Any new appointee—especially an internal appointee—must negotiate for the authority to make necessary organizational changes, including personnel changes. Too often an insider accepts a job and comes to find his or her hands are tied in dealing with a difficult employee. Once appointed to the leadership position, the successful internal candidate has many advantages. She knows the organization, the successes, the challenges, the personnel, the budget, the politics, and the key people in the organization. And the people know the new leader. That familiarity can also be a disadvantage as people may expect a certain status quo for a while. Relationships established with colleagues in other units may need to change as the new leader interacts in a new way with new responsibilities. The new leader must project that new role immediately and consistently.

Former colleagues will face a new working relationship with a former peer who is now a leader and supervisor. There may be a certain aloofness or tension between parties for a while as each evaluates the other in the new role. Even the most generous and supportive of colleagues will find it awkward for a while. There may be a need for negotiation to establish support from colleagues who did not endorse the search committee's selection and who could undermine the library administration. The wise leader will pay special attention to key colleagues, bringing them into the planning and into conversations about the vision of the unit. All colleagues, particularly those who may have been opposed to the candidate—or may have been competitors—need to believe there is room for them, their ideas, and their growth in the new administration. The astute leader will parlay any competitiveness from ambitious or dissatisfied colleagues into projects or new job responsibilities developed to serve the needs of these individuals while furthering the unit's vision and purpose.

CAMPUS PARTNERSHIPS AND LEADERSHIP

Relationships with colleagues across the institution also need to change to reflect the new leadership role. The new leader represents the interests of the unit as a whole and is in the position to interact with other unit heads as a peer. Strong partnerships already forged can now be enhanced by the authority to set goals, to commit resources, or to build support for shared projects. The new leader can and must ensure that the library is getting the best services and support from other units. This may require positive but clear assertion with people who are used to seeing her in a different role. The new leader's demeanor must reflect her leadership role in the university; a buddy-buddy relationship may not be appropriate for the level of discourse in which she will be engaged.

A new leader needs to move forward on changes and improvements. The successful internal candidate may find it more difficult because people may balk at accepting unpopular decisions from someone they "used to know and like." Many former peers may not see the need to "prove themselves" to her; they may believe the ball is in her court concerning what might affect them. The organization as a whole may not expect big changes right away. Ideally, the new leader has used the interview process effectively to showcase new ideas and plans that indicate a fresh, independent approach that will engage the organization and everyone in the process. Once appointed, the new leader must repeat these goals and approaches at every opportunity.

Ultimately, the new leader sets a tone and a direction for the organization. The successful leader creates an atmosphere that encourages shared values and the commitment of the organization. It is the shared vision for the future that serves as a focus for the new administration. Noel Tichy and Eli Cohen discuss how leadership involves telling a story about the organization that engages followers and sets a vision for the future (1997: 172–173). Successful internal candidates can be story-tellers for their organizations. Familiarity with the institution creates the opportunity to draw on experience, knowledge, and working relationships to describe the work and mission of the organization throughout and beyond the campus.

The successful internal candidate can embrace all the advantages of being an "insider" while using the hiring process to project a worldly vision for the future and to negotiate for the unit. Those doing the hiring should know her priorities and should expect that changes and innovation are likely. The successful new leader also will gauge the political capital available and expend it appropriately to strengthen and promote the organization and institution.

REFERENCES

Dowdall, Jean. 2000. "Does the Internal Candidate Have the Edge?" *The Chronicle of Higher Education* (April 7, 2000) [Online edition]. Available: *http://chronicle.com.jobs/2000/04/2000040701C.htm4/7/2000*. [23 October 2001].

Kaplan, Gary. 1999. "Now what? The Pros and Cons of Hiring from Within or Without." *ACA News* 42, no. 9: 8–9.

Mason, Julie Cohen. 1992. "In the Market for a New Boss?" *Management Review* 81, no. 10: 10.

Overman, Stephanie. 1994. "Hiring: The Inside Track." *HR Magazine* 39, no. 9: 54.

Tichy, Noel and Eli Cohen. 1997. *The Leadership Engine: How Winning Companies Build Leaders at Every Level*. New York: HarperBusiness.

Part V

Anticipating What's Next: Leadership for Digital Initiatives

Chapter 11

Considering Leadership and the New Architecture for Digital Libraries

Barbara I. Dewey
Dean of Libraries and Professor, University of Tennessee

The conception, creation, and sustenance of digital libraries is a growing concern to a variety of stakeholders in the academy. In many ways, digital libraries symbolize an important visible result of the intense collaboration and partnership activities characteristic of the new leadership described in this book. Creation of digital libraries requires not only new ways of working cooperatively but also different organizational models to accommodate diverse campus cultures. Digital libraries are really metaphors for new higher education models and the leadership they will require for successful implementation. This chapter examines the new architecture for digital libraries and the resulting imperative for innovative models of teaching, research, and accompanying support services as well as implications for campus leadership, drawing on themes from previous chapters in *Leadership, Higher Education, and the Information Age: A New Era for Information Technology and Libraries*.

THE EMERGING DIGITAL LIBRARY

What is a digital library? Many interpretations can be found within the academic community. Borgman notes that, "in general, researchers view digital libraries as content collected on behalf of user communities, while practicing librarians view digital libraries as institutions or services" (1999: 227). Suleman and Fox note that digital libraries are at the intersection of library science, computer science, and networked information resources (2001). Research and practice are occurring simultaneously in the digital library arena, contributing even more to the divergent definitions. Digital libraries in the current context include reformatted digital content originating from library materials in traditional formats or from other sources, commercially available digital resources, content that was originally presented in digital form (commonly known as born-digital content), and digital services that connect resources with users.

The new digital library architecture encompasses not only a wide variety of content but services and communication features as well. More than content, the emerging digital library also contains an interactive and collaborative component. Tochtermann talks about building the communication aspect of digital libraries to mirror the collaborative and highly interactive use of traditional libraries (1996). The digital library as a device for communication including accompanying services between faculty, students, and others is now a reality through chat rooms, electronic mail, interactive learning environments, and the like. The digital library is also more ubiquitous in the lab, the classroom, dorms, and faculty offices. The content of the new digital library is much broader than the traditional set of scholarly journals, reports, books, and other commonly held physical objects.

Components of the digital library have been around for many years beginning with online catalogs, emerging electronic databases and publications, and the tools to access these materials from a discipline-based point of view. Although some aspects of the digital library parallel the traditional library model, such as selection, dissemination, and preservation, the notion of a comprehensive digital library really took off with the advent of the Internet and the World Wide Web. The ability to network electronic resources offered greater exposure of and accessibility to scholarly material not readily available in the traditional print-based library. These developments also spawned the need for a variety of access tools and service models to assist people in locating and using digital materials.

DIGITAL LIBRARY PARTICIPANTS: LOCAL AND GLOBAL

The digital library, like the traditional library, includes a major human component. However, unlike the traditional library, where librarians worked in a largely independent fashion, the digital library's existence requires the convergence of many participants. They include librarians, technologists, information scientists, students, faculty, and campus administrators. How universities leverage the expertise of these participants will determine the success, robustness, and sustainability of digital libraries in higher education.

The digital library is a bit like a series of concentric circles. It can have a core local component but is also part of a mega–digital library spanning the globe. The blurring of institutional ownership and borders is a primary feature of the Web-based digital library. Key participants may well be located beyond a particular campus. Implementers of the local digital library often seek partners from other universities or institutions, taking advantage of complementary technical expertise and unique content from across the globe.

BUILDING STANDARDS FOR DIGITAL LIBRARY DEVELOPMENT

Membership organizations such as the Coalition for Networked Information (CNI) and the Digital Library Federation (DLF) provide support for development and implementation of digital library standards essential for the new, more integrated digital library architecture, as well as partnership possibilities. The Digital Library Federation uses endorsements to promote attention to standards and best practices of its members; for example, it recently endorsed principles developed by the Institute of Museum and Library Services (IMLS) for digital collections emphasizing the need for useful content and interoperability (www.imls.gov/pubs/forumframework.htm [8 April 2002]) and (www.diglib.org/standards/imlsframe.htm [8 April 2002]).

The application of best practices and standards is the hallmark of a successful digital library. Attention to standards will ensure that the digital library will grow in a coordinated fashion rather than in separate content areas. Interoperability with other digital library collections is based on the use of widely recognized standards. However, the new digital architecture is constantly evolving, and available standards are not always "ready" to accept the content and services creative campus leadership wishes to include. As a result, digital library creators need to incorporate experimentation in the architectural rendering to ensure inclusion of the most innovative and useful content. Appropriate standards development is, therefore, content driven and must be flexible and robust enough to incorporate the constant stream of new content.

FUNDING THE DIGITAL LIBRARY

Colleges and universities embarking on library digital work generally secure grant support for individual projects and then begin to integrate costs into existing operating budgets. External funding sources for digital library development is a major consideration in launching the initiatives. Representative external funding sources include the Institute for Museum and Library Services grant programs, the National Science Foundation, and the Mellon Foundation. Local and regional foundations may be a possibility for funding projects related to those geographic areas. Experimental and innovative applications for digital library development are often the most successful projects for external funding.

Sustaining digital library development costs money, which ultimately must come from a variety of sources. Though many efforts begin with grant funding of one sort or another, sustainable digital libraries must have at least some funding that is part of an institution's ongoing budget. Staffing, equipment, and workspace are all necessary components. Libraries and IT organizations often look within their existing budgets to reallocate funds, equipment, people, and space to do the work of the digital library. The most challenging ongoing need is the sustaining production work (scanning, software application, and the like). A creative approach to staffing and the development of a solid business and operational plan are essential for a successful long-term effort.

THE INTEGRATED DIGITAL LIBRARY

Early digital library development has been largely a local, project-based endeavor. Projects have focused on digitizing collections of unique materials, often in isolation of the institution's other information assets and of other similar digital collections found elsewhere. Typically the work is done by a few library staff. The end result can be found on the library's Web page, oftentimes isolated from other collections and resources owned by the library. The digital library is defined solely by the digitized collections. Funding is typically through a grant or some other nonrecurring budget source. Selection of digitized collections is often determined by the funding source rather than by other standard collection selection strategies.

While isolated project-based digital library developments have been crucial for launching an institution's program, new approaches and strategies are emerging. The new architecture for the digital library is integrated rather than isolated. It is comprehensive rather than singular. Development is accomplished in institutionwide teams rather than by the library alone. Work is integrated into the operations of the university rather than undertaken as a special side function. Funding is conceived as an integral part of the institution's budget. Content from all parts of the university is considered in a broad sense, including digital as well as commercial resources. Virtual interactive services are included. Seamless, comprehensive, and discipline-based access to the digital library is the goal instead of chance access through a single point of entry. The creation of dynamic learning as well as teaching environments is becoming part of digital library development.

THE SCHOLARS PORTAL CONCEPT

Campbell describes the new integrated digital library through the scholars portal concept.

> The *scholars portal* would facilitate the addition of high-quality material by fostering standards, searching across databases, and offering a variety of supporting tools. As a result, libraries, corporations, and many other organizations would be empowered to contribute to an accessible, distributed digital library. The existence and efforts of *scholars portal*, therefore, would accelerate the growth of high-quality material and facilitate what has been referred to as the global relational research library. (Campbell, 2000)

Campbell's concept is one that is being embraced, at least in part, on many campuses. The notion of a digital library that transcends a local online catalog with a smattering of reformatted digital collections is taking hold. The scholars portal concept puts a face on the new integrated digital library and provides a context for concrete development of such capabilities.

Another view of the portal concept has been developed by Sarah Thomas, University Librarian at Cornell. She describes the ideal discovery tool as "one which consults omnivorously, but which returns a selection of relevant results in rapid sequence. Searchers find what they need promptly without having to wade through a vast assortment of tangentially related, inaccurate, or otherwise deficient data"(Thomas, 2000). Thomas's imaginary tool, largely a combination of powerful portal and search engine, is the basis of a powerful digital library.

Conceptualizing the digital library in one's imagination is a great thing, but reality is better. The implications of a scholars portal underscores the integrated future of digital library development. The successful creation of a workable portal will involve technologists, librarians, and faculty on local campuses as well as commercial vendors. Several major entities are currently working on bringing the reality of the scholars portal to fruition. The concept has grown to match the new architectural model of an integrated library. Initially focused on content, services are now a part of the desired portal. The Association of Research Libraries (ARL) has established a working group to develop ways to bring together content and service. At the same time, integrated library system vendors are also bringing customized cross-searching capability to the marketplace. Lastly, researchers from information sciences, computer sciences, engineering, and other areas continue to develop innovative tools and applications that relate to the digital library.

EVOLUTION OF THE NEW DIGITAL LIBRARY ARCHITECTURE: CURRENT CONTEXT

Aspects of the new library architecture are already in place on most college and university campuses. The online catalog, commercial electronic databases, full-text journals, electronic books, data sets, reformatted collections, and preselected scholarly Web sites constitute the content aspect of the digital library. Figure 1 is a graphic example of the University of Tennessee's emerging digital library universe.

The library online catalog, now Web-based, provides a gateway for some of the scholarly resources "owned" by universities and colleges. More recently it appears as a link on the library's homepage. In the case of the University of Tennessee, several online catalogs make up the digital library environment—UT's catalog, the Kudzu catalog (linking resources of 16 southeastern libraries), catalogs of the Oak Ridge National Laboratory, and other UT campuses. Simultaneous searching is possible across some of these catalogs.

The integrated digital library also contains commercially produced research databases, electronic journals, electronic book collections, and other digital materials of scholarly or teaching value available from publishers. The integration of commercial and locally produced content is a challenge for the new digital library. Because of license agreements, some of its content must be restricted to campus users and requires authentication. Com-

Figure 1

Digital Initiatives of the University of Tennessee Libraries

UT Libraries Web Site—**www.lib.utk.edu**
Gateway to information available locally or via the Internet

AskUs.Now Virtual Reference Service
- Service at place and time convenient to user needs
- Video conferencing for remote reference service to support distance education

Integrated Library System
- Online Catalog **Since 1986**
- Acquisitions, Serials check-in, Circulation, self check-out

IRIS Virtual Catalog
Materials from the Information Alliance libraries: University of Tennessee, University of Kentucky, and Vanderbilt University—including delivery **Since 1998**

UT Song Index
Location information for more than 50,000 songs **Created in 1981, online since 1995**

Manuscript Finding Aids
Electronic access to unique documents in Special Collections

UT Digital Library Center **Funded Summer 2001**

Southeastern Native American Documents
Institute of Museum and Library Services project with the University of Georgia Libraries, McClung Museum, and Tennessee State Library **1999 - 2001**

Virtual Collection of Great Smoky Mountain Photographs
- Roth Collection Sampler

Digital Library Federation Member
- Digitized Galston-Busoni Music Collection **1993-1994**
- Participant in DLF/Mellon digital library proposal

ASERL KUDZU Library Project
Virtual catalog and document delivery from 16 major Southeastern Research Libraries

Research Support
- Networked Electronic Resources:
  - Full-text Databases
  - Electronic Journals
  - Citation Databases
  - E-books
  - Online Reference Books
  - Aggregator Services
  - Numeric Databases
  - Government Documents
  - Cartographic Materials
- Key player in advocacy for Tennessee Electronic Library
- E-journals listed in the online catalog

Online Course Reserves for UT Students
Digitized articles, chapters, and faculty-created study materials **Regular service began Fall 2000**

The Studio
Digital multimedia laboratory for students and faculty **Fall 2001**

Digital Media Service **Summer 2001**
- Digitizing service to support online instruction
- Cooperative effort with OIT

Data Services Department
Provides access to datafiles for secondary analysis

Library Instructional Services Online
- Tutorials for First Year Studies, English, Agriculture
- Streamed video for Business reference sources
- Web catalog tutorial
- Video Tour

Information Access and Document Delivery
- ILLiad management system for online requests, reporting, fax delivery **Fall 2000**
- Document delivery via subsidized access to faxed journal articles **Since 1997**
- Online requests for document delivery to campus offices

Scholarly Communication
- Copyright website for faculty — **www.lib.utk.edu/plan/copyrt/**
- Electronic Theses and Dissertations Project
- Future plans for scholarly e-publishing

Updated August 2001

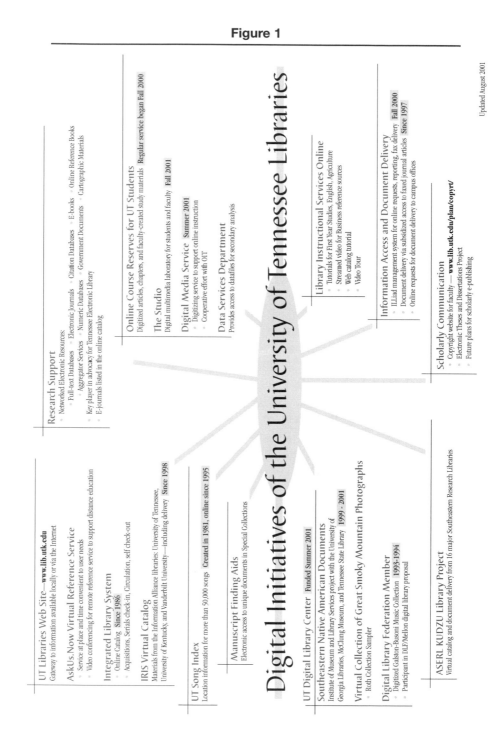

mercial content is often located at remote servers. Cross-platform searching is challenging. However, the new digital library architecture seeks to embrace fluid access to commercial content as well as to locally owned and produced content.

Increasingly scholarly resources are located beyond even the newer Web-based library catalogs. They are not "owned" by the library in the traditional sense. However, some subject-based Web sites are preselected by librarians and collected in some fashion on the library Web site. Customized search tools such as manuscript finding aids and boutique indexes are also found somewhere on the library Web site. These resources are not well integrated into libraries' catalog searching capabilities, nor are they easy to find from general Web search engines.

The presence of reformatted digital collections developed by the individual library, usually rare or unique items from special collections departments, is a newer part of the digital library configuration. Also emerging are cooperative digitizing projects such as AmericanSouth.org, a project of the Association of Academic Southeastern Research Libraries (ASERL), where cohesive subject-based special collections (often with regional themes) are pulled together by several institutions. Consortial or membership organizations' collections of digital objects such as the Digital Library Federation are linked in some way using developing standards. Currently these collections are found somewhere on the institution's Web site but are not well integrated with the online catalog.

SERVICING THE DIGITAL LIBRARY

Services are an increasingly important part of effectively linking users to the exploding amount of content in the campus digital library. Examples include electronic reserves, synchronous and asynchronous virtual reference and consultation, electronic document fulfillment and delivery, online user instruction, and multimedia creation. The huge amount of information, scholarly resources, and media points to a growing need for online services to assist users in finding what they need when they need it.

Access to electronic reserves is one of the earlier digital services emerging on the digital library scene, even though it was originally conceived in isolation and in advance of the comprehensive digital library concept. Most colleges and universities of any size have extensive electronic reserve operations featuring text. A few institutions are serving up images, video, and audio to the classroom. Production is a major challenge for electronic reserve operations. To address this challenge, institutions are seeking commercially or consortially produced content such as image and audio archives. This is particularly true with efforts to provide images traditionally owned only in slide libraries. Of course a host of intellectual property and copyright issues accompany the transformation of multimedia formats to digital Web-based formats.

Virtual reference services are rapidly appearing on library Web sites around the world. These services enable a library user to query a librarian with questions about the digital library content (or traditional library content). Although electronic mail reference service is common, more and more libraries are now featuring some kind of interactive or chat service where the user can "talk" directly to a librarian in real time. The ability to offer such a service on a 24/7 basis truly requires worldwide participation to cover all time zones and areas of expertise. Alternatively some libraries are staffing their operations 24/7 to address queries with local staff. Regardless of the implementation process, users can communicate directly with experts in the new digital library architecture.

The existence of services in the new digital libraries also provides more interaction about the curriculum among librarians, technologists, faculty, and students. Both the content and the services can be imbedded, for example, in course Web pages. Librarians and academic computing staff need to work closely with faculty to make this happen. Students are more likely to use high quality scholarly resources if they have a direct link to the library from course Web pages. They are more likely to seek assistance if virtual reference services or help desk functions are easy to access. Interactive instructional modules for specific course-related databases or for instruction on how to select quality Web resources can also be available directly from the course Web site.

CAPTURING CAMPUS COLLECTIONS AND SERVICES

The new digital library goes beyond traditional library boundaries and embraces collegiate or department-based digital resources and services of importance to students and faculty. Identifying rich campuswide resources currently sitting in isolation of potential local and remote users is a great challenge made more possible by Web-based formats. These resources include everything from image collections, digitized map data, specialized indexes, art portfolios, and technical report literature. Creators often want these materials to be widely available but need a more integrated campus initiative to make that happen.

CREATING SCHOLARLY RESOURCES IN THE NEW DIGITAL LIBRARY ENVIRONMENT

The new digital library architecture is dynamic and interactive. Creation of new knowledge directly by the author for the reader or by using an electronic scholarly publishing process constitutes a new dimension for library content and usage. Librarians and technologists can work together to develop ways for the creator of content to make it available to the campus and beyond. An example is the University of Iowa's Bailiwick, a Web space for research-based Web publications, where authors retain full editorial control of their content and "where academic passions can be realized" (www.bailiwick.lib.uiowa.edu). California Polytechnic features a system where faculty can deposit research reports or other scholarly works in electronic format with appropriate metadata so the material can be accessed. The University of Michigan is producing a large number of "born-digital" journals. The ability to create and deposit scholarly output and engage in electronic publishing offers a new, transformational role for colleges and universities in the scholarly communication process.

SPACE NEEDS FOR DIGITAL LIBRARY WORK

Creating and contributing digital library content and applying it to research and teaching requires physical as well as virtual space. A collaborative and partnership spirit is particularly important in creating the spaces needed to harness the power of the digital library. Innovative spaces are being developed on many campuses where students, faculty, librarians, and technologists create content, digitize it in a variety of formats, and put together multimedia scholarship and presentations. These spaces are also used to apply learning technologies for curriculum development; for example, in instructional and lab space. The successful collaborative physical space for digital work emerges from new partnerships among librarians, technologists, and faculty. A Web site featuring examples of best practices for collaborative spaces has been developed by the Coalition for Networked Information in partnership with Dartmouth College. The new digital library creates innovative spaces where expertise, content, and sheer creativity come together in a powerful environment for teaching and learning.

DIGITAL LIBRARY DEVELOPMENT: AN ASSESSMENT

The state of digital libraries is opportunistic and immature. Most activity related to digitizing collections remains project based and grant funded rather than fully integrated into the life of the library or campus. Many efforts are focused primarily if not exclusively on library resources, although other campus developments are also taking place. The output of these nonlibrary efforts is not yet fully integrated into the online catalog or made available through a powerful Web-based search strategy. All aspects of staffing for the digital library effort are under development, including training needs, workforce configuration, job creation, and integration into the work of the campus. Campus collaboration is becoming more common, and the creation of multiple federated digital libraries, including national and international coordination of efforts, is a major goal.

Universities are working towards the new integrated library architecture using a collaborative approach. Some notable examples include MIT's Dspace (http://web.mit.edu/dspace/), a digital archive created to capture and distribute the intellectual output of MIT. Dspace is a joint project of MIT Libraries and the Hewlett-Packard Company and provides the stable long-term storage needed to house the approximately ten thousand articles produced annually by MIT faculty and researchers. Cornell University's Cornell Institute for Digital Collections is another example of bringing together digital products and resources from across the campus. The California Digital Library (www.cdlib.org/) and OhioLink (www.ohiolink.edu/) are the most comprehensive statewide efforts to broadly deploy digital library content from many institutions and commercial entities. Other states are developing virtual libraries featuring a smorgasbord of digital content and services.

Typically universities are at the forefront of such initiatives. How are universities doing with digital library development? To answer this question, a survey was sent to all Association for Research Libraries members. Of the 35 respondents, 34 are currently pursuing digital library initiatives.

Organizational issues. The way universities organize their digitization efforts becomes increasingly important as the application of digital library collections and services becomes more integrated into the life of the university. In the survey, 12 institutions reported decentralized structure, 9 reported centralized structure, and 14 reported a combination type of structure. While many of the mature, large digital library efforts are centralized with an actual department in the library populated with specialists, many libraries are beginning to move in the direction of decentralization, so that these efforts can become part of day-to-day operations. An example is to have metadata and tagging activities emanate from the library's technical services (cataloging) department, technological aspects of the system contributed by library systems and campus IT departments, and selection of materials to be digitized or included carried out by subject librarians and faculty.

Campus partners. This existence of partners in the development of the campus digital library is growing. Examples cited by survey respondents included:

- Campuswide steering committees
- Advisory boards

- Statewide advisory groups
- Statewide management structure
- Coordinating committees
- Ad hoc committees for specific projects
- Specialized IT groups
- Librarians
- Faculty
- Academic technology departments
- Academic departments
- Graduate colleges (especially for electronic thesis and dissertation work)

Partners were identified by 26 of the respondents by word of mouth or prior contact. Nine institutions indicated use of a "call for participation" mechanism to increase involvement and locate appropriate campus projects not previously known by library staff.

Project selection. Once partners are identified, how are projects selected? Criteria noted by respondents included:

- Relevance to teaching and/or research (26)
- Selection by library staff (30)
- Selection by an advisory or steering committee (15)
- Funding availability (27)

Respondents could mark more than one of the criteria. Other criteria that were noted included the strategy of capitalizing on collection strengths and expertise of faculty and staff. The existence of institution-based internal grant programs sometimes uncovers relevant projects. The state of the data or original material and whether it contains any descriptive data or metadata can be important criteria. The feasibility of bringing the material through a reasonable workflow also includes meeting technical and legal criteria (copyright and digital rights management issues). Many projects are simply identified through personal initiative by librarians, technologists, and/or faculty and are largely opportunistic. Lastly, the public relations value of a topic is a potential reason for implementation. The emerging digital library is opportunistic and immature, so direct connections to research and teaching are not always as strong as they should be in project selection.

Search engine capability. Although 18 institutions indicated a robust search capability for their digital library initiatives, none actually exhibited this capability in reality from their Web site. No institution, at the time of the survey, had the capability of offering the researcher the ability to bring together scholarly materials digitized locally (including from other parts of the campus) and resources from the online catalog, scholarly Web sites, and commercial databases available to that particular institution. A researcher cannot find articles on bluebells, songs about bluebells, Web sites dealing with bluebells, images of bluebells, streaming video of bluebells, and curricular resources to teach about bluebells within one search.

The robust searching capability is really the crux of the new digital library architecture. While current developments are impressive, many features of the new integrated digital library are still emerging. For example, a digital library gateway for the University of Tennessee would include library resources, services, and instruction. The gateway would sit on a comprehensive campus Web site with a powerful search engine. Through the gateway, students and faculty would gain access to library resources, services, and collegiate-based digital scholarly resources held in academic departments, faculty offices, and research laboratories. Seamless access to the resources of collaborative facilities such as the Oak Ridge National Laboratory, specialized databases found in large research centers, and data from agricultural experiment stations would be available. Faculty and instructors would have tools to link to resources from course Web sites as well as to the virtual services. The gateway and the UT Web site would provide integrated subject-based searching across the various collections. The development of such a gateway is a leadership imperative for the new digital library.

LEADERSHIP CHALLENGES FOR THE NEW DIGITAL LIBRARY

Identifying and locating digital content from across the campus (and beyond) for both teaching and learning remains a major challenge for the new digital library. Success requires active and persistent partnerships between faculty, librarians, and technologists where communication of new projects and resources is ongoing. A side benefit of such close collaboration is a more cohesive campus culture based on many bridges across traditional discipline and profession-based silos.

Incorporating learning and teaching resources as an integral part of the digital library constitutes an important and rather new challenge. To date, most digital library initiatives ignore curricular materials and interactive teaching/learning aids such as Web-based tutorials. These materials exist online but are not part of a comprehensive architecture. Colleges and universities are currently making major investments in course management systems, mechanisms for digitizing course content, and distance education efforts relying on digital course content and resource delivery. Furthermore, the imperative to integrate the use of appropriate research materials in the learning process is strong, in part to capitalize on the huge investment made in purchasing commercial electronic databases and journals and in digitizing local materials. Appropriate integration of curricular resources should be a key part of a campus digital library program. Additionally, national efforts to collect online course-related materials such as MERLOT should be linked to local digital libraries.

The existence of a robust search engine that effectively crosses the boundaries among traditional, electronic, instructional, and curricular educational resources combined with links to appropriate services is an essential component of the new digital library. Whether called a scholarly portal or gateway, this super search engine does not yet exist. Its development and implementation rely on collaborative leadership among librarians, technologists, and faculty (especially researchers in disciplines such as computer, information, and engineering sciences).

The implementation of powerful cross-institutional search

capabilities is another crucial element in the new digital library architecture. Knowledge and expertise go beyond institutional boundaries. Therefore new digital library architecture must have the capacity to reach deeply into existing scholarship, regardless of its source. Harnessing the power of organizations devoted to developing digital libraries—such as the Digital Library Federation, EDUCAUSE, the Association for Research Libraries, educational consortia such as the Committee on Institutional Cooperation (CIC) and the Big Twelve, plus international, regional, and state organizations—is central to an institution's digital library efforts. The development of new knowledge is a global endeavor, and our campus structures must provide links to international scholarship. Fortunately the application of new technologies has broken down many of the barriers that existed in the past for a more extended reach to global scholarly resources and services.

NEXT STEPS IN THE NEW DIGITAL LIBRARY DEVELOPMENT

The issues of broad resource identification, including both research and teaching materials, robust and cross-institutional search engine development, and integration of global resources and services, will pave the way for a truly integrated campus digital library. On a national level, new systems are being developed to answer the issues of powerful searching of digital material. New development of the scholarly portal concept is also showing promise. Application of digitizing standards and searching protocols has become a reality. Forays into creation and production of scholarly resources are more commonplace. All of these initiatives need to be woven together into the integrated digital library.

Partnerships and collaboration among campus stakeholders, as well as with national and international coalitions, are making the next steps for new digital library development happen. The new era of leadership is all about the ability to work within several cultures, just as digital library development is all about working within several formats or media. The imperative for collaboration has never been stronger, because, without all of the players, the integrated digital library will not emerge. New leadership must be not only collaborative but also creative and strategic in approach and outcome. For higher education in the twenty-first century, the new digital library architecture will bring together the power of research and teaching in a form never seen before. Constantly evolving, the new digital library will broaden access to the fruits of scholarship to the world, bringing the world to the campus and the campus to the world.

Leaders from the library, the IT organization, faculty, and central administration are coming together to build the new digital library. This new era of leadership demands a collaborative, creative, and strategic approach for advancing higher education in the complex global twenty-first century.

REFERENCES

Borgman, Christine. 1999. "What Are Digital Libraries? Competing Visions." *Information Processing and Management* 35: 222–243.

Campbell, Jerry D. 2000. "The Case for Creating a Scholars Portal to the Web: A White Paper." *ARL Bimonthly Newsletter* Issue 211 (August). [Online]. Available: *www.arl.org/newsltr/211/portal*. [8 April 2002].

Suleman, Hussein, and Edward A. Fox. 2001. "A Framework for Building Open Digital Libraries." D-Lib Magazine 7: 12. [Online]. Available: *www.dlib.org/dlib/december01/Suleman/12Suleman*. [8 April 2002].

Thomas, Sarah E. 2000. "Abundance, Attention, and Access: Of Portals and Catalogs." *ARL Bimonthly Newsletter* Issue 212 (October 2000). [Online]. Available: *www.arl.org/newslt/212*. [8 April 2002].

Tochtermann, Klaus. 1996. A First Step Toward Communication in Virtual Libraries. *Technical Report, Center for the Study of Digital Libraries, Texas A & M University*. [Online]. Available: *www.csdl.tamu.edu/csdl/pubs/klaus/TecRepKlaus*. [8April 2002].

Index

E

F

G

About the Frye Leadership Institute

Authors of this collection first came together in June 2000 as part of the Inaugural Class of the Frye Leadership Institute in Atlanta, Georgia. Named for Billy E. Frye, Chancellor Emeritus of Emory University, the annual program is primarily supported by a grant from the Robert W. Woodruff Foundation and sponsored by EDUCAUSE, the Council on Library and Information Resources (CLIR), and Emory University to respond to an increasing need for strategic and wise leadership of information resources in higher education. Motivated by Frye's vision and inspired by his courage and compassion, Brian Hawkins (EDUCAUSE President), Patricia Battin (first President of the Commission on Preservation Access), and Deanna Marcum (President of CLIR) supported the development of an intensive two-week program for selected leaders of higher education .

Our class of 43 professionals included 28 women and 15 men from a range of public and private institutions, with approximately equal representation from colleges, community colleges, and universities. We represented 25 geographically dispersed states, Canada, The Netherlands, and England. The group included faculty and academic administrators, for example, Associate Deans; University Librarians and Associate Librarians; and IT leaders, most of whom held director-level positions; several held joint faculty/technology appointments. We were diverse in our ages and life experience, including a few participants in their early thirties up through Baby Boomers in the fifty-something range.

The Institute offered an opportunity to explore a wide range of information resources issues in higher education through readings and presentations by experts, probing conversations with these experts and, throughout, animated dialog among the participants. Institute Deans Deanna Marcum and Richard Detweiler (President of Hartwick College), gracefully guided discourse and debate as the group tackled challenging issues facing concerned professionals today—such as scholarly communications, public policy, and intellectual property, especially as they affect and interact with higher education.

All of the contributing authors of this collection were inspired by their explorations of issues in academic leadership at the Frye Leadership Institute. The experience led to a great deal of strategic thinking and inquiry, as *Leadership, Higher Education, and the Information Age: A New Era for Information Technology and Libraries* reflects. The gift of insight and camaraderie encouraged confidence in our ability to provide the kind of transformational leadership that each "new era" of higher education will require. We hope that readers will feel the spark of creativity, ingenuity, and inspiration as well.

Carrie E. Regenstein
University of Wisconsin-Madison

About the Contributors

ANNE SCRIVENER AGEE is Executive Director of the Division of Instructional and Technology Support Services and Deputy Chief Information Officer at George Mason University. She is responsible for coordinating the University's technology integration initiatives, including program planning and faculty and student support and training. In particular, she has worked with the College of Arts and Sciences at George Mason University to develop the Technology Across the Curriculum program, winner of the 2001's EDUCAUSE award for Systemic Progress in Teaching and Learning. She holds an M.A. in English from Ohio University and a doctorate in rhetoric from the Catholic University of America.

LOIS BROOKS is the Director of Stanford University's Academic Computing group, which provides technology-based services and resources to students, faculty, and staff. She has worked at Stanford for many years, focusing on the effective use of technology in learning, teaching, and work processes.

JO ANN CARR has been the Director of the Center for Instructional Materials and Computing at the School of Education, University of Wisconsin-Madison since 1984. A graduate from Indiana University (B.A. 1973, M.L.S. 1974) she has published and presented extensively on the topics of information literacy, curriculum center management, electronic resources in education, and teacher education reform. A charter member of the National Education Network Executive Committee, Ms. Carr was named the 1999 Distinguished Education and Behavioral Sciences Librarian by the Association of College and Research Libraries.

BARBARA I. DEWEY has been Dean of Libraries at the University of Tennessee, Knoxville, since August of 2000, when she left the University of Iowa, where she held a number of administrative positions including Acting University Librarian and Director of Information and Research Services. She was also Director of Admissions and Placement, Indiana University School of Library and Information Sciences, Reference and Interlibrary Loan Librarian, Northwestern University, and Head of Reference, Minnesota Valley Regional Library, Mankato, Minnesota. Dewey has an M.A. in Library Science and a B.A. in Anthropology and Sociology from the University of Minnesota. She has published and made presentations on digital libraries, library fund raising, personnel administration, public services, and information technology applications in research libraries and is an active member of national and international research library organizations.

RENEE DRABIER is the Chief Technology Officer and Director of Information Technology Services at the University of Southern Colorado. Her doctorate was awarded in 1997 by Texas A&M University, College of Education. Her M.B.A. was earned at the University of Texas at San Antonio in 1987, and her bachelor's degree is in Music Education/Music Therapy from the University of Kansas, 1976. Dr. Drabier is responsible for the establishment and management of the Instructional Technology Center at the University of Southern Colorado, which is funded in part by a U.S. Department of Education grant. She spent 14 years at the University of Texas Health Sciences Center at San Antonio prior to moving to the University of Southern Colorado, where she managed a distance-learning program and was recognized by the United States Distance Education Association for the "Most Outstanding Distance Learning Network for 1992." Her program was also given written commendation by the Alabama Board of Nursing for "Excellence in planning and development for distance learning," December 1994.

CHRIS FERGUSON, Dean for Information Resources at Pacific Lutheran University, provides leadership for library, academic and administrative computing, telecommunications, and audio, television, and multimedia services. Previous positions include executive director for an integrated library-computing organization at the University of Southern California and director of USC's Leavey Library, which created the nation's first information commons. Dr. Ferguson has published several articles on library services and the next generation of (integrated) information services.

JAY FERN is the Manager of Online Learning for Indiana University Purdue University Indianapolis (IUPUI). Fern received his D.M.A. in Music Education at the University of Southern California with special emphasis on the application of technology to music instruction. He earned a M.M. in Music Education at the University of Nevada–Reno and a B.M.E. at Murray State University in Kentucky. As manager of Online Learning, Dr. Fern coordinates and manages Oncourse: Indiana University's premier Online Teaching and Learning Environment. In addition, he is co-author of a multicultural music series—"Global Voices in Song." The CD-ROM series explores the aural music traditions of cultures such as South Africa, Hungary, Japan, and New Zealand. Recently, Dr. Fern was the Interim Director of the Indiana Learning Collaborative, which he brought to fruition through a partnership of IUPUI and Indiana cultural institutions. He is frequently invited to speak at educational institutions regarding course management systems as well as at music-related conferences throughout the country and internationally.

ELIZABETH D. HAMMOND is Dean of the University Libraries at Mercer University, responsible for general library services on the Macon and Atlanta campuses and for Extended Education Library Services. She also serves as Dean of the Division of Library Services. A native of Illinois, Ms. Hammond received her B.A. in Art History and M.L.S. from the University of Illinois at Urbana-Champaign. At Mercer University, she held previous positions in circulation, reference, collection development, and library administration before being selected dean in 1999. Ms. Hammond has served ACRL as Chapters Council President and in a number of other committee assignments. Her current research interests are leadership issues in higher education, library-faculty collaboration, and library services for diverse user populations.

DEE ANN HOLISKY is Associate Dean for Academic Programs in the College of Arts and Sciences at George Mason University. A faculty member at George Mason since 1980, Dr. Holisky is an Associate Professor of Linguistics and a past director of Linguistics Programs. Her research specialty is languages of the Caucasus, and she has published on Georgian, Tsova-Tush, English grammar for ESL teachers, and vocabulary for ESL students. She earned her Ph.D. in linguistics from the University of Chicago.

C. PATRICK KOHRMAN II designed and fills the position of Chief Information Officer for the Berks-Lehigh Valley College of Penn State University. He has 20 years experience as an instructor in business administration and has been teaching in the areas of business statistics and management information systems. Mr. Kohrman has been instrumental in establishing IT strategic planning for the college, implementing a lifecycling plan, standardizing the college computing platform, and most recently, has led the expansion of instructional design services at the college. He has written distance education course materials and also teaches for the World Campus of Penn State University. Mr. Kohrman has served as a project manager in the development of BerksNet, a countrywide intranet and continues to be involved in community projects. Pat is also an alumnus of the inaugural Frye Institute. He received his B.A. in Economics from Susquehanna University and his M.B.A. from Penn State University.

TERRY METZ recently assumed the newly created position of College Librarian and Associate Vice President for Information Technology and Services at Wheaton College in Norton, Massachusetts. For the prior decade he served various roles in the library and computing units at Carleton College, including interim appointments as College Librarian and Director of Administration Computing. Mr. Metz received B.A. degrees in business administration and geography from Gustavus Adophus College in 1980, and an M.A. in library science from the University of Minnesota in 1985. From 1986 to 1992 he served as Consortium Manager for Cooperating Libraries Consortium (CLIC), a non-profit consortium of seven private liberal arts college libraries in the Minneapolis/St. Paul area. Prior to working for CLIC, he was employed as a librarian at Hamline University in St. Paul.

Anne Murray currently holds the post of Deputy Librarian at Cambridge University Library, England. Her library career began in special libraries and included posts at FAS, the Training and Employment Authority in Dublin, Ireland, and Coopers & Lybrand in London, England. Her academic career began at Dublin City University (DCU), in Ireland. There she held two posts, first, Assistant Librarian, Collection Development, and then Sub-Librarian, Planning and Budgets. While working at DCU Anne also completed an M.A. in Communication and Cultural Studies. She then moved to Trinity College Dublin where she took up the post of Sub-Librarian, Collection Management, before returning to the United Kingdom to take up her current post at Cambridge in 2000. Anne's professional interests include library service quality and the management of change. She led the DCU Library quality initiative that resulted in its being the first library in Ireland to be awarded the Q-Mark by Excellence Ireland. She has presented papers in England and Ireland on quality service initiatives within the library environment.

Pattie Orr is the Director of User Services for Wellesley College in Wellesley, Massachusetts. She joined the Wellesley College Information Services Department in July 1992. As the Director of User Services, she and her staff oversee all aspects of user support including college public computer labs, Wellesley DormNet, Wellesley HelpDesk, as well as Technology Training/ Education and all computing documentation. Pattie teaches courses and conducts workshops about software applications for faculty, staff, and students. Over the past three years, Pattie has worked with the Boston Consortium to form a vendor partnership with Element K in order to bring online training to all

Wellesley faculty, staff, and students. She is also involved in IT management consulting, providing consulting for colleges in on-site meetings, workshops, and working groups. Her areas of expertise include user support reorganization, library/IT integration, creating self-reliance in users, and designing a user support matrix for residential computing. Prior to her arrival at Wellesley, she spent ten years teaching and supporting instructional technology in secondary and higher education in both Texas and Massachusetts. Ms. Orr holds a Master of Education from Lesley College (Cambridge, MA), focusing her research on the effect of residential computing on higher education. She is involved in many professional associations, including EDUCAUSE, CLAC, and NERCOMP. She serves on the NERCOMP's Board of Trustees.

Carrie E. Regenstein became the Associate CIO/Director of DoIT (Division of Information Technology) at the University of Wisconsin-Madison in June of 2001. Prior to that, she served as Director of Academic Technology Services (a unit of Information Technology Services) and Assistant Dean for Educational Technology for the college at the University of Rochester, after many years of leading academic technology initiatives at Cornell University. Regenstein regularly contributes nationally in leadership and teaching capacities in the information technology arena in higher education. In 2002, she accepted an invitation to join the Advisory Committee of the Institute for Computer Policy and Law, jointly sponsored by EDUCAUSE and Cornell University.

Robert Renaud is Director of the Waidner-Spahr Library and Associate Dean of the College at Dickinson College in Carlisle, Pennsylvania. He has held positions in computing and library services at Connecticut College, the University of Toronto, McGill University, the Metropolitan Toronto Reference Library, and the University of Arizona. His related experience includes work on technical standards of organizations, EDUCAUSE, and the American Library Association. He holds a B.A. in history from Vassar College and an M.L.S. from the University of Toronto.

VINCE SHEEHAN is Chief Information Officer and Associate Dean for Information Technology at the Indiana University School of Medicine. He has 25 years experience in information services management, having worked in city government, banking, and healthcare before joining Indiana University three years ago. His area of focus is building organizations and decision-making processes to effectively deliver information technology services. Sheehan recently led the development of a Strategic Technology Plan for the Indiana University School of Medicine. He has a B.A. in Religious Studies from Indiana University.

DENNIS A. TRINKLE is Associate Coordinator of Information Services and Technology and Tenzer Family University Professor in Instructional Technology at DePauw University. He also serves as Executive Director of the American Association for History and Computing. Dr. Trinkle received his M.A. and Ph.D. from the University of Cincinnati. His previous books include *History.edu: Essays on Teaching with Technology, The History Highway 2000,* and *Writing, Teaching, and Researching History in the Electronic Age: Historians and Computers.*